Time Management Mama:
Making Use of the Margins to
Pursue Your Passions

Sarah Korhnak
Beth Anne Schwamberger

Cover Design by Katy Campbell of LittleRedFlag.Etsy.com

First Edition: May 2015

ACKNOWLEDGEMENTS

This book would not have been possible without the help of so many talented, brilliant women who were willing to pore over our very rough drafts and iterations and give their encouragement, feedback, and critical eye to make the content on these pages infinitely better.

To Mom: You've always been our biggest cheerleader and the sounding board we so desperately need. Not only did you lend your critical eye to our first drafts, you also played a crucial role in combining the feedback of the other editors. You were our editor-in-chief, and in so many ways, you've served as "Editor-in-Chief" of our lives as well. You're the voice of reason, the cautionary word given with kindness and empathy, the collector of our memories, the encourager and the soft place to land, and somehow, you've refined each of your children and grand-children into beautiful "first editions". We love you, Mom!

To Katy: You not only designed our cover, but set the tone for our planner, and, let's be honest, the course of our brand. You took our million ideas on design and condensed them down to a beautiful, cohesive product. You are so kind, patient, and intuitive.

To Victoria: Is it strange to call you our biggest fan? You're not only that *(which, to us, feels like the greatest honor we could receive!)* but you're also a wonderful friend. Our common love of Anne Bogel led you to us, and you've been such a joyful blessing ever since. Keep on writing and sharing your voice - it's a beautiful one. Someday, we'll all meet in real life, and it will be the BEST!

To Kate: You are all brilliance and no-nonsense gathered beneath a slew of gorgeous red hair. Your matter-of-factness was just what we needed when the editing got tough! Thank you for giving your precious time to this project.

To Carla: Your positive, sweet spirit shines through in every interaction you have. You were thorough. You invested so much time in your edits, despite being new to our community. We're so lucky to know you!

To Diane: Your insightful comments on this book have been a gem! Thank you for being such a great friend and supporter of my dreams. I am so grateful for our friendship.

To Julie: You have always been a great encourager

of my business goals, and I really appreciate the time you spent critiquing this book. I am so glad we have been friends for so many years. I know I can always count on you despite the distance that separates us.

To Jessica: You are one-of-a-kind, and you make the lives of everyone who knows you more fun and unique. I treasure our friendship along with your independent spirit. It's been wonderful to have a fellow freedom-fighter nearby to be in cahoots with. Keep going. You got this.

To Melissa: You're the glue of the Brilliant Business Moms Community. Though your hands didn't touch this book directly, they've touched it in so many ways through the wisdom and encouragement you offer to us all.

To Jill: I admire you so much, dear friend. Your support has been a treasure.

DEDICATION

To my dear husband Mike and my 3 wonderful children - Lilly, Charity, and Sullivan: You are the reason I can and do, dream big dreams. Thank you for your unwavering support and encouragement. Your patience through my perseverance has not been overlooked. I love you all more than words can say.

To Chris: My biggest supporter and the man who so generously gives me lots of margin to pursue all my passions, including you, Holden, and Brilliant Business Moms. You're continually positive, never stop believing I can make things happen, and the hardest working human being I know. I'll never understand how I snagged you, but thank you for being mine.

To Holden: You're the reason my time matters infinitely more than it used to. My days are full of more laughter, more fun, and fabulous new ways of seeing the world since you came into my life. The time I have with you - it's priceless sweet boy.

TABLE OF CONTENTS

INTRODUCTION

Hey there! It's so nice to meet you! We want you to know that we're honored that you've picked up our book. Giving a little bit of your time to us is no small gift. We don't want to waste it.

Since there are many examples in the book of how we've used time management in our own lives, we should probably introduce ourselves to give you a little bit of context.

We're Sarah Korhnak and Beth Anne Schwamberger. We're sisters, moms, and we're constantly dreaming big dreams in the midst of the more mundane parts of our day. Sarah is the nerdy, practical type with a degree in accounting. She has 3 kids ranging from 8 to 4 years old and she's married to Mike, the kindest most mild-natured accountant you'll ever meet! Beth Anne is a bit more dramatic and is a Registered Nurse by trade. She has one son, Holden who is four years old and is married to Chris, the goofiest fighter jet pilot you'll ever meet!

In 2012, we started an Etsy shop called The Amateur Naturalist where we sell butterfly terrarium kits. By 2013, Beth Anne was listening to podcasts constantly to gain ideas on how to grow the butterfly terrarium business. Then it dawned on her; there are no podcasts out there geared toward moms in our situation; trying to grow a new business while raising great kids. This revelation resulted in a frantic phone call to Sarah "I know what we have to do!" And so, without any technical knowledge about podcasting or background in communications, the Brilliant Business Moms podcast was born on June 10th, 2014. Each week we interview a new mamapreneur to glean great business and personal advice -- all geared toward moms who are starting a business from their kitchen table.

The one thing we're most proud of is the community of talented, smart, encouraging women that we've gathered together through our podcast and website. Everyone on our email list is given an invite to join our private Facebook group, and our group members love it because of the genuine connection and advice they receive there. We certainly can't take all the credit for this. Each week, we sit back, amazed at the incredible women who are brought into the group! We're so grateful for them!

When you hear us mention our "Brilliant Business Moms Community" this is what we're referring to. Throughout the book, members of our community have chimed in with their own great advice on time management and pursing their passions as a mom. Of course, it doesn't seem very nice to mention this "exclusive group" without giving you the chance to join. We'd absolutely love to have you along! You can head to BrilliantBusinessMoms.com/TMM to sign up and receive an invite.

In several places throughout the book, we've included examples of planner pages that help us to stay organized or accomplish a particular goal. To grab your own free copies of our pages, you can head to BrilliantBusinessMoms.com/TMM and you'll be emailed a link and a password for a secret page on our site with all the worksheets in the book available for download.

We feel like moms have unique struggles in growing a business that we try to address. We understand where they are coming from, because that is where we are now! If you're not a mom, we welcome you too! And if you're not trying to start a business, the takeaways can be applicable to any endeavor you are taking on! We hope this book allows you to find more joy in your every-day tasks, get things done faster, and steal away bits of time to pursue the things you're most passionate about.

Who is Time Management Mama for and what can it do to help?

Productivity is hard. Accomplishing big goals is even harder, and trying to grow a business or pursue a great big goal while raising kids feels almost impossible!

This book is for those of us who are mixing motherhood with other passions. We are raising babies while working tirelessly at an enormous goal. We are playing with preschoolers while pursuing our passions. It is difficult enough to manage a home and love on our children without adding impossible dreams to the mix. But we know you can do it, and this book can help!

As a mamapreneur, being productive in the home is just as important as being productive with your business. The two go hand in hand because we juggle the kids, the home, and the business all day long. Using our time wisely in one area inevitably helps the other areas as well.

We don't have the luxury of a 9-5 schedule where we can work exclusively on our business or big dream. Many of us are choosing to stay home with our kids and build our dream business in the snatches of time we find between carpools, bottles, and play dough.

Others of us still work a traditional 9-5 job, so our margins in the hours-off must be balanced wisely to have time for our families as well as time to pursue other passions. The exhaustion of a 9-5 job fuels the fire for building a business where we can be our own boss.

As moms, it's not possible to simply cross the home-front off the list and move on. Meals, laundry, and cleaning can't be put off indefinitely. Our families are more pleasant when they are fed, clean, and not living in filth.

We get it. We live there.

We've drawn from our own experiences,

trials, and errors when writing this book. We type not from corner offices and conference rooms but from crusty couches and crumb-filled kitchens. We've gathered the best tips from other moms in the trenches too. So you'll hear not only what works for us, but what works for them too. This book is full of strategies used by real moms that help them to be as productive as possible in their day-to-day lives. When used together, these strategies will give you the margins you need to pursue your biggest passions instead of letting another year pass by wondering, "what if..."

If you are not a mom, we welcome you too! Many of the strategies discussed in this book will apply to you as well, but there may be a few chapters you'll want to skip over.

What This Book is Not

This book is not an easy fix. Reading it won't bestow upon you a magic potion for getting five times as much done each day. It won't tell you step-by-step how to finish that home remodel or get your first 1,000 sales. But by putting the words on these pages into action you can absolutely find the time and tools to finish those great big goals of yours.

This book is not a self-help book. We're not

going to get "woo-woo" on you and ask you to journal your biggest fears or darkest secrets. While we do share snippets of our lives and our faith as we illustrate what we've learned about productivity, we're not touchy-feely storytellers. We're practical, and we're action-takers. If this book is in your hands, we believe that you are too.

You're already talented, smart, loving, and kind. You're a great mom, a caring spouse, and a woman on a mission. Your life is probably pretty great already. You just need a few practical tips to fill in the gaps and make better use of those blessed margins.

"Sarah and Beth Anne" I can hear you saying, "there are so many books out there on productivity. What makes you two so special?"

That's a great question! We're not special. That's the beauty of this book. We're regular moms, just like you. We have young children at home. We juggle school projects and play dates, sick days and rainy days, the household schedule and our biggest hopes and dreams. There's a lack of excellent, balanced advice for moms in the trenches, especially moms like us who are trying to build a business or make a big dream a reality. We feel depressed when we read productivity and business books written by dudes for dudes.

Here's Some of THEIR Advice

Spend 4 hours first thing in the morning working on your biggest goal!

(Umm... and who is watching the kids.....?)

Work towards your goal with reckless abandon. Go all in!!!

(Umm... and who's going to pay for my kids' counseling when they feel neglected, unimportant, and unloved?)

Outsource all the unimportant tasks!

(With what budget? The pennies I find under the couch cushion?)

Push yourself further than you've ever pushed before!

(Oh wait... you mean further than that time I pushed a human being out of my body?)

If you don't double your income and triple your customers in 6 months, you're a failure. Go big or go home.

(I'm pretty proud of myself for putting my children

first each day. I'm proud of the beautiful, happy, loving home I've created. That's not failure – that's success of the highest order.)

Our advice acknowledges the unique and important position you have in life – your job as MOM. No earthly position comes before this difficult, beautiful, priceless role. We know that each day looks a little different for you, and they're all ruled by chocolate milk-mustachioed dictators and sticky-fingered preschool presidents. It is possible to keep trudging on in the trenches of motherhood while carving out time for other goals, hopes and dreams. They all deserve a place at the table.

We are moms with big dreams, just like you, and that, more than anything else, qualifies us to write a book that is for you.

We hope you enjoy it. We hope you find some areas for change and improvement. Most of all, we hope you'll continue to pursue your passions right along with your biggest role as Mom.

So what are we waiting for? Let's dig in!

~ Sarah Korhnak & Beth Anne Schwamberger

Chapter 1: Your Top 5 Passions and Goals
-Beth Anne

What are your biggest goals this year? Are you ready to write that book, start that blog, lose twenty pounds, run a marathon, get a promotion or learn to knit? If you're anything like me, your list of goals often includes several noble pursuits.

"Absolutely," I tell myself. "I can be a great mom, military spouse, volunteer at church, eat healthier every day, do more craft projects, be my son's physical therapist, read more books, run a marathon, start a new Etsy shop, write a book, save enough money for our second adoption, and grow a blog to 100,000 visitors/month in one year. **Of course I can do all that and more!"**

By the end of January each year, I'm left with a half-finished scarf, rotten veggies in the fridge, a budget that's anything but balanced, a new shop with just two, puny little listings, and a cranky husband and son because mommy is overwhelmed and has no time for them. Of course, I've also gained weight from all the added stress. **Does your goal-setting process sound anything like mine?**

This year, I'm determined to do things differently.   I'm choosing true passions over surface pursuits.   I'm focusing only on what matters most. I hope you'll join me!

There's a story about a famous business man providing counsel to one of his employees that goes something like this: He asks the employee to thoughtfully list the twenty-five goals which are most important to him. The man dutifully writes down his top twenty-five goals. They're all worthy pursuits and quite important to him. [1]

For our purposes, we'll ask: What are the most important items you want to accomplish in the next 12 months?   If that feels too overwhelming, start with the passions you'd like to pursue in the next 3 months, instead.

Next, the business man asks his employee to pick only his top five most important goals. This task seems nearly impossible. Every item on the list is important. After some thought, the man narrows his list. He's quite excited at this point and eager to get started on pursuing his passions and finally accomplishing his top goals.

Here's the kicker: When the employee is asked about what he'll do with the other twenty things that had once been on his list, he tells his boss that they're still important goals.... that he'll work on them intermittently between the bigger goals. He'll tackle them when he can.

Here's the secret that so many of us busy, yet passionate mamas miss: Those other twenty things are no longer good things.... They've just become your worst enemy. Those twenty things are your "**do not do at any cost**" list.

What's the big deal? Weren't those twenty things a close second to your top five biggest passions and goals? Couldn't you have easily picked number six on your list instead of number four? Why would you now avoid that item?

The reason those twenty items have now been demoted to your "do not do" list is **because good is the enemy of best**. Too many choices and distractions will paralyze you into doing nothing... or into doing everything halfway. Think about your business goals for a minute. There's no good way to turn a profit on a half finished product or a half written book.

Before you venture any further into this book, it's critical that you determine your top five passions and goals. It's impossible to have razor sharp focus and accomplish your goals if you're still unsure of what they are. Take a few minutes or even a few hours to brainstorm the top twenty-five most important goals you'd like to accomplish in the next year. These can be personal goals, relationship goals, parenting goals, business or blogging goals - you name it!

If you'd like to do the exercise I'm about to outline, you can head to BrilliantBusinessMoms.com/TMM to grab our goal-setting worksheets. ready? Let's go!

Write down the areas of your life that you're most passionate about. For you, this could be your writing, being a mom, your career - you name it! From there, write down the goals within each area that you'd like to accomplish in the next

12 months. Initially, you'll just be brain-dumping. Write down everything that sounds like a great idea - both big and small.

Below is my example of how I used the 25 Things Worksheet.

What I'd Like To Do + What Matters Most

Run a half marathon at an 8:30 pace
Weekend getaway with Chris
Join a small group Bible study
Write a book on time-management for moms
Pinterest Team → Group Board - Joint Strategy
Online conference for mom biz owners/bloggers
Host a brilliant business moms meet up/one day event
Study the Bible daily
Lose 10 pounds
Work with Holden on PT 30 min/day
Week-long family vacation
Volunteer for Children's ministry
Create an online course → Pinterest advertising → Etsy SEO
Read 1 hour to Holden each day
Learn a new Bible verse w/ Holden each week
Grow email list to 15,000 subscribers
Add 30 new listings to Etsy Shop
Create a printable planner for Etsy Sellers
Give Chris' encouragement daily
Eat 5 fruits + veggies a day
Weekly date w/ Chris
Teach Holden to read
Grow business to be profitable w/ Sarah + I ea. making part-time income
Grow podcast to 30,000 downloads per month
Host a backyard Bible Camp
Create an audio book
1-on-1 coaching program? Learn fb ads

Use this page to brainstorm everything you would like to do this year along with all of your top priorities and passions. Don't overthink it, just start writing!

Finally, once you're armed with your list of at

least 25 items, it's time to dig deep and eliminate all but your most important goals - the ones that keep you up at night and get you excited to start your day - the goals that will allow you to make a difference in your little corner of the world.

Below is my example of breaking down my top 5 passions and top 5 goals.

My Top 5 Passions + Goals

1. **PASSION** My Faith / Jesus → **GOAL** Read the Bible daily

2. **PASSION** My Marriage → **GOAL** Words of affirmation / appreciation / encouragement to Chris daily

3. **PASSION** Motherhood → **GOAL** Spend quality time w/ Holden daily. Distraction-free play time + story time. Laugh often ☺

4. **PASSION** Brilliant Business Moms → **GOAL** Income Growth - take home part-time salary by the end of 2015

5. **PASSION** Health / Physical Fitness → **GOAL** exercise daily - even if it's only 5 min. - build a daily habit

It's tempting to tackle everything on the list you just made, but you'll spread yourself too thin if you attempt them all. Start by solidifying your top 5 passions then choose just one most important goal for each.

My Top 5 Areas of Passion are:

- My Faith
- My Marriage
- Motherhood
- Growing a Business
- My Health & Well-Being

Based on those passions, I'll share my top 5 goals for the next 12 months.

- Read something from the Bible each day.
- Speak words of affirmation to my husband Chris every day.
- Spend focused, one-on-one play time with Holden each day. Laugh with him, love on him, and connect with him.
- Grow our business to be profitable, with Sarah and I each taking home a part-time salary from our endeavors.
- Exercise every day.

Several of my goals are more about building habits than they are about any huge, audacious dream. Your top five goals might look very different. Maybe you're committed to completing a triathlon, homeschooling five children, and growing your blog to one million readers. That's amazing! Go for it!

In my life, I've noticed that small steps over time add up to significant changes. I'm starting small, yet intentional with my goals. The next twelve months for me, are most focused on building priceless habits. You may already be a person of many habits. *(Did I mention that you're amazing?!)* Please don't feel the need to replicate my goals. You can go much bigger or much smaller. This exercise is all about what's most important and vital for you in the next twelve months. What are your passions? What are the big goals you want to accomplish in pursuit of those passions?

If you have several daily habit goals like I do, here's a word of encouragement: Once you establish those new goals as true daily habits, you can move on to new goals while retaining the old ones. However, if you start out with five additional goals of eating ten fruits and veggies a day, cooking only with whole foods, spending an hour a day in quiet time, completing a triathlon, writing a love note to your husband every day, and more... there's a good chance that none of those goals will turn into meaningful habits. Focus in on just one key goal for each passion. You can absolutely add more goals later once you've kicked your first set of five in the pants!

One of the most helpful things for me during this exercise was figuring out what I wanted most for our business - The Brilliant Business Moms brand - which consists of a podcast, a blog, and far too many product ideas! What was most important to accomplish this year? Did I care about more website traffic or podcast listeners? Did I want to write a certain number of posts or interview some key guests? Did I want to grow social media to certain levels? Did I want to connect and encourage more moms? *(a definite yes!)* When I looked at all the possibilities, I realized that income growth was at the top of the list.

This might sound shallow. The standard advice is to give like crazy, help as many people as you can and the money will follow. I absolutely agree with that advice. However, I think that sentiment is more applicable to those who have a tendency to forget about people and focus only on dollar signs. For Sarah and I, a financial plan and goals for the business are more difficult to keep in the forefront of our minds. More often than not, this seems to be the case for women. We give and help all the time. Yet, sometimes, we forget that in order to keep doing the amazing work we're doing, we have to make some money doing it.

What is your big goal for the next twelve months? Out of all the ideas and "nice-to-do" things that you jotted down, what's the one goal that stood out as being most important? Keeping that one big goal in mind will give you the focus and follow-through you need to pursue it, meet it, and hopefully, surpass it!

Deciding on income growth as our main business goal gave me a razor sharp focus in breaking down that goal into the baby steps needed to complete it. I'll teach you how to break down your big goal in chapter 2.

When I'm tempted to spend time learning more about a particular form of social media or improving my photography, I'm reminded of my main goal right now – income growth. I ask myself, "What is the fastest, most efficient way to achieve my most important goal?"

Once you have decided on your most important goal for each of your passions, there will be other goals that did not make the list. As an example, below are some items that did not make my list this year:

- Go on a nice, long family vacation.
- Run a half marathon at an 8:30 pace.
- Work on a collaborative Pinterest project

- Teach my son Holden how to read

(I realize that last goal seems super important, but Holden is 4 years old, so if it doesn't happen this year, he's still doing just fine!)

It may feel like a total downer to look at all the items you crossed off of your list and know that they may not happen this year. They were worthy goals to pursue. They would have been fun and enjoyable. You would have felt amazing after you accomplished them! I can feel your irritated stare through the pages, "C'mon, Beth Anne, don't be such a kill-joy here!"

What I hope you'll discover as you read this book, is that one of the biggest kill-joys we face as moms is being too busy, too distracted, and just plain overwhelmed. When we set the best things as our goals and focus on them with absolute resolve, there will be plenty of leisure time left to help others, build relationships, and live a year full of fun, laughter, and few regrets. Let's forget about all of those "good" distractions until our best goals are accomplished. And with that kind of focus, you'll be able to cross off these goals in six months and start fresh with five new goals to conquer! I have a feeling you're about to crush it, and I can't wait to see it happen!

Take-Aways

- Write down your Top 5 Passions
- Write down every possible, nice-to-do goal within that area of passion. No need to edit yourself here, just brain-dump everything that you'd love to achieve or habits you'd like to create
- Spend some time in careful thought to determine what your top goal within each area of passion will be.
- Pursue that goal with reckless abandon. Eliminate everything else on the list. Choose best over good, and make things happen!

Chapter 2: Get your Ph.D. in Specificity
-Beth Anne

In Chapter 1, we chose our five areas of passion and then zeroed in on the goals that would help us to pursue them.

We started with twenty-five things that we'd like to do, and whittled them down to just five essential goals. Hopefully, one of those five goals is something huge! It's a dream you've wanted to pursue for a while. It's a blog you've been dying to start, a new line of pottery you want to create, or a revenue goal for your business that feels a bit daring.

Once we determine our big goal – that great

big plan of ours that we want to achieve in the next twelve months, we need to break it down into much smaller projects and tasks. Don't make the mistake of keeping your to-do list vague. For example, if you want to grow your blog audience by ten thousand readers per month, it's going to require writing more content, and killer content at that. So every week, "blog posts" will find their way onto your list.

Should you just keep it at that, though? Perhaps you have a few ideas swimming around in your head. Why not just wait until you have two uninterrupted hours to sit down, mull over your topic, and start writing?

Let me give you an example to illustrate why this may not be the best idea.

Have you ever told your preschooler, "It's time to get dressed"! "Ok, Mommy", you hear a pleasant voice shout back. Thirty minutes later, you walk into your preschooler's room to find him in his undies with his sneakers on, struggling to pull his jeans up over his shoes. His shirt is on backwards and inside out, and....by the way, he's covered in a mysterious pink goo that's completely ruined his outfit of choice. "Seriously... where is all of this candy coming from?" you wonder, "and will he ever finish a lollipop all in one sitting?"

Fortunately, I have the answers: The candy is coming from the grandparents and that kid at preschool with the lumpy pockets; and no, he will **never** finish a lollipop in one sitting. Just let that dream die right now. I'll give you a moment of silence to grieve.

Sometimes our brains can be just like that well-intentioned preschooler: believing they can do it, but easily distracted and often turning that project into a sticky mess without a firm plan.

Maybe your brain is way more advanced than my preschooler version, but when I give myself the vague task of writing a blog post, this is what happens: I peruse Facebook and Twitter to see what my favorite business bloggers are writing about. "Oh wait, my friend just posted family photos...oh my goodness, how cute are those? I guess it would be okay if I spent just a few minutes on Pinterest looking for photo prop ideas. I mean I have it on my to-do list to get some new family photos...."

One hour later, I've got some great family photo ideas, several new recipes to try, and new outfits that I just have to have. "Oh no!" I look at the clock and realize that I have one hour left to get this post researched, written, polished, and published. I frantically write run-on sentences, misspell several words, and format the post in a way that makes no sense. I snag a random photo, add some text, and voila!

The result: This post is nothing groundbreaking. I was rushed. I didn't have enough time to approach anything from a new angle. A few readers may pop over and take a look, but no one will be sharing this one. No one will care enough to comment. It's been done before.

So what went wrong in the scenario above?

I failed to break down my project into small, detailed tasks. I failed to remember that my brain will snatch up every chance it can get to veer off course.

The Importance of Being Specific

The directions we give ourselves should look more like the ones we give to our preschoolers:

Just as a preschooler who is new to dressing himself needs steps like this:

1. Take off your PJ pants
2. Take off your socks
3. Put on your new socks
4. Put on your new pants
5. Take off your shirt
6. Put on your new shirt.
7. Comb   and   smooth   your   hair

When trying to complete a great blog post, my easily-distracted brain needs steps like this:

1. Decide on a discussion topic
2. Write an outline of the key points you want to include
3. Fill in each point with anecdotes and how-to's
4. Write a compelling intro that places your reader in the story
5. Create a post title that's short, to-the-point, but interesting
6. Create a gorgeous cover photo with title overlaid
7. Spell-check, format, and complete SEO *(search engine optimization)* for the post

Within this list, many of these steps can be broken down even further. Perhaps you need to research and cite sources for your post. This is a separate point. In order to Create a cover photo you may have to hunt for a stock photo, download, upload to your photo editing program, add text, and crop it to the right size.

Be specific with each task on your list. This will keep you focused. There's no room for wandering onto Facebook or into your Inbox when you have your outline in front of you, and the next job is clearly laid out. The simpler you get, the easier it is to follow-through.

Step-by-Step: Accomplish Your Goal

Below is an example of accomplishing a much larger goal. Let's suppose you're working on a new project: launching a podcast. Which list of tasks will help you to efficiently accomplish your goal?

List 1: Launch a podcast for moms who have small businesses while spending time with their children

OR

1. Decide on a title and tagline for your mom business podcast
2. Purchase a domain name

3. Set up Web Hosting, Wordpress, Genesis, and purchase a Site Theme. *(This is actually four separate steps!)*
4. Find ten business moms to ask for an interview
5. Pick three moms you already know so you can get a few yes's under your belt
6. Listen to several other interview-style podcasts and then decide on the questions you will ask in each of your episodes
7. Draft your "ask email" including an intro, the things you admire about that business mom, some answers to frequently asked questions, the timeline, potential dates for the interview, and the questions you'd like to ask
8. Practice interviews with friends until you figure out Skype Recording
9. Research and order microphones for you and your co-host.
10. Research recording and editing software.

11. Nail down sound quality for your guests. What equipment and software do they need?

12. Do a test group Skype call with Sarah, Beth Anne, and Mom to test software and sound quality.

13. After the test call, hone your recording strategy.

14. Schedule five interviews in advance

15. Record the intro episode

16. Write an intro blog post

17. Set up accounts on social media

18. Set up an email account

19. Edit the first few episodes

20. Write show notes for each episode

21. Create cover photos for each episode

22. Sign up for a podcast-hosting service

23. Buy an ID3 editor to tag podcast episodes

24. Create the podcast cover art

25. Tag the first 3 podcast episodes and upload to the podcast hosting service

26. Submit the podcast feed to podcast directories such as iTunes

27. Launch!!!

I bet you didn't think it would take twenty-seven steps or more to start and launch a podcast. The second list looks more overwhelming than the first and may even dissuade you from getting started. However, the second, more detailed list makes the project realistic. You're beginning with a clear picture of everything that must be accomplished and in what order. Step by step, day after day, as you go through each task on the list, you'll accomplish your goal. *(And your brain will thank you!)*

It's All in the List

You can set a due date for your Big Goal and work backwards to determine the due date for each step, or you can realistically estimate how long each step will take, and work forward to set a due date based on that estimate. Either way, having firm deadlines and someone to hold you accountable is key. I'll discuss that more in Chapter 7.

If you choose to follow a detailed list to complete your big goal, you may miss out on some things. There's a good chance you'll have no idea what everyone is talking about on Facebook. You may miss out on some marketing tips from your favorite online business guru. You'll have less hearts on your posted-less-often

Instagram photos. However, you will have completed a big goal that you're passionate about. It's completely your choice. If you'd rather have the latter *(and let's face it, we could look at cute pictures of your kids on Insta all day!)* that's completely fine. Every choice we make, both big and small, has a trade-off.

For Sarah and I, following a detailed list to launch the Brilliant Business Moms Podcast has provided the opportunity to meet some of the most amazing, talented moms on the planet. Encouraging other moms, making online friends who share our passions and priorities, learning and growing from the support we receive in our community, and feeling that we get to make a difference - these experiences would have been missed. That's not a trade-off we were willing to make. The podcast took a lot of work and planning to launch, but it has been so worth it!

What is your biggest goal this year?

Whether it's creating a new product line, launching a blog, growing your customer base, or increasing revenue, there are many little steps necessary to help you get there.

Take time today to brainstorm the steps involved in reaching your big goal. That single goal will quickly turn into five smaller goals, and each of those may involve five more steps. Keep breaking down your tasks until they're as specific as possible. You may have to organize and re-organize your list so that it makes sense and flows logically.

Leave space to add and revise your list as you work, but whatever you do: **make that list!** That simple piece of paper could change your life.

On the following page are examples of how I've used our Big Goal Breakdown worksheets this year. They're not pretty, but they absolutely work. And these sheets are just the beginning. Each big goal has been broken down into multiple more sheets to get specific, give myself deadlines, and make things happen.

Big Goal Mind-Mapping

recurring → 3,000 revenue customers in 2015

Planner for Etsy Sellers + Mom Bloggers

webinars

Advertising Strategy

— Instagram
2 giveaways per month
fb

Promoted pins   twitter

ebook, Time Mgmt. for Moms.

Audiobook
Self-produced

mini course
on turning
ebook into
Audiobook

↓

50 course
Sales 2015

Income
Growth →
Accelerated +
low Start Up
Funds

use ebook to build list

↓

free printables from planner
for opt-in

→ Ultimate-bundles

Blogger Reviews

Goal = 50 Reviews/
Giveaways

Affiliate
Program

ebook
marketing

Etsy Shop
to White Etsy
SEO for planner

Give copy
to all
past
Interviewees

→ 100 Amazon Reviews
from our Community

apply to Bookbub
+ Book Buds

This is another way to map out your big goal. Write down everything you can think of and add spokes and bubbles to make connections.

Grab your own worksheets when you sign up for our list by visiting BrilliantBusinessMoms.com/TMM.

Take-Aways

- Break down your big goal into bite-size steps.
- Create small, detailed tasks to accomplish to make it easier for your brain to focus and complete a project.
- Small tasks make progress possible versus one big goal which can often feel overwhelming.
- You can do this! Break down that goal, then get to work.

Chapter 3: Take Charge Of Your Time
-Sarah

I first learned about the concept of time blocking from reading Amy Lynn Andrews' book *Tell Your Time.* [2] The concept is a simple one, but quite profound. The idea she presents in her book is that for each chunk of our day we need to map out what we will be doing in order to be most productive. Basically you schedule your entire day, but leave in some wiggle room as well. By time blocking, you also ensure that the most important things are scheduled in first. Time blocking will help you begin thinking about how to spend and schedule your time each day.

I began with a detailed model of time blocking my days but have gradually settled on a more general system. Even though my time blocking is broad, it still helps me to plan what I should be doing with my time. It erases the question, "What should I do next?"

Time blocking also addresses the prioritizing of household items and business items. How do you pick between a blog post deadline and doing laundry? How do you decide if scheduling podcast interviews should take precedence over a quick sweep and vacuum? Time blocking has helped me solve some of those conundrums. My default is often to gravitate towards business work, but time blocking helps me to schedule household tasks as well. Because I have laid out the plan, I don't feel guilty if I am sweeping the floor instead of writing, or editing an interview instead of vacuuming.

Let me explain how my time blocking system works: My time blocking changes as things at home change, especially the children's schedule. This year Lilly is in second grade, Charity is in afternoon kindergarten, and Sullivan is in preschool two mornings a week. Each day until about 8:45, my mornings are occupied with getting ready for the day; showering, dressing, eating breakfast, and heading to the bus stop.

Three mornings a week we are home, so one morning I will usually block time for laundry, another morning will be household tasks and cleaning, and the third morning will be set aside for the business. Preschool mornings are usually time blocked for errands because the stores are near the school. Each day, 11:00-12:00 is blocked to get Charity ready for school, feed her lunch, and wait for her bus. From 12:00 to 12:30 I have my lunch break. I like to eat lunch while I listen to part of an audio book or podcast -- it's a little indulgence of mine!

After lunch, Sullivan has a quiet time and I dive into the work I need to do for the business. After Sullivan is done with his quiet time, it is still my work time until the girls get home from school at 3:45. Sullivan knows that the afternoon is mommy's work time, and he does a pretty good job of letting me work while he plays. There are interruptions for sure, but in general, I can get through quite a bit of work in the afternoon with only one child at home. Usually I stop work at 3:20 so that Sullivan and I can play and read together, just the two of us, before the girls get home. Sullivan knows that if he plays on his own while I work in the afternoons that I will reserve that time for just the two of us to play.

When the girls get home, I put work aside, greet them, look at the papers flying out of their backpacks and listen to the stories about their day.

The rest of the evening is usually consumed with dinner prep, dinner, kitchen clean-up, homework, kids' activities, baths, and family time.

When the kids go to bed, I do light business work such as reading emails, because I'm too drained for anything more taxing, followed by a Netflix show.

This is the area where Beth Anne and I really differ. Beth Anne has tons of energy at night and often works from 9-11PM on the business. I can barely stand to look at a computer screen by the evening!

On the following page is my example of how I've time-blocked my general weekly schedule:

Time Block a Typical Week

	MONDAY	TUESDAY	WEDNESDAY	THURSDAY	FRIDAY	SATURDAY	SUNDAY
5							
6	Get Up Exercise Get Ready						Get Up Get Ready
7							
8	Get Kids Ready						
9	Business Work	Preschool Drop Errands	Household Tasks	Preschool Drop Errands	Laundry	Kids Activities	Church
10							
11	Kids Lunch Ready for School My Lunch	Charity Lunch Preschool Pickup Sullivan Lunch My Lunch	Kids Lunch Ready for School My Lunch	Charity lunch Preschool Pickup Sullivan Lunch My Lunch	Kids lunch Ready for School My Lunch		Lunch
12	Brilliant Business Moms Work	My Lunch		My Lunch			
1		work time	work time	work time	work time		
2							Family Time
3							
4	Household and Family	Household and Family	Household and Family	Household and Family	Household and Family	Family Time and Kids Activities	
5	Dinner	Dinner	Dinner	Dinner	Dinner		
6	Girl Scouts	Family Time	Girls Dance		Family Time		
7				Soccer Practice			
8	Kids in Bed						
9	Light Work Relax!						

When you sign up at BriliantBusinessMoms.com/TMM you can snag your own blank time-blocking worksheet to use.

My time blocking schedule is broad, but there is a schedule and a pattern. I hardly ever do housework during my afternoon work time, and I hardly ever do business items during my late afternoon and evening family and house time. A general schedule like this really helps me to not feel guilty about doing one thing over another and provides me with a balance of priorities. An added bonus is that I'm not flopping back and forth between activities. I assign the largest possible chunks of time to the intended task.

One other point to mention, because of my To Do list which I'll discuss further in Chapter 4, I already know which big item I will tackle during my business time. If you are a mom at home with babies I would recommend blocking off the quietest part of your day to tackle your major business tasks or to pursue your passion. Don't check email, just dive into that big item on your To Do list. Fill in the rest of your schedule with smaller tasks. You may be able to grab small blocks of business time throughout the day, but make a plan for those large chunks. Fill in your remaining time with home and baby.

If you are a working mom trying to grow your business or pursue a hobby after work hours, most likely your best blocks of time would either be early in the morning, in the evening after the kids go to bed, or on weekends.

Block time for your business and passions when you feel at your best. I am a morning person--

not a night owl. Beth Anne is the opposite. Schedule your business block of time for when you have energy and motivation, but make sure you use that time to tackle your major item, not just respond to email or Facebook. Save email, social media, and other less demanding details for another time when you are not at your best.

Every person will have their own, unique time-blocking schedule based upon obligations that can't be changed, when the kids are at home, work schedules and energy levels.

As you begin to time block your schedule, don't forget to block in time for family, fun, and friends! These are priorities too, and by scheduling them, you won't worry about taking time away from work or chores. Scheduled fun puts your mind at ease. You've planned for fun and you can look forward to it while you're busy working.

Take-Aways
- Set up a system for time blocking, and ensure that all of your priorities have a designated time during your week.
- Time blocking allows you to know what you should be doing and when. This puts your mind at ease and lets you fully focus on the task at hand.

Chapter 4: How to Turn the Dreaded To Do List Into A Delight! -Sarah

Now that you have your day segmented into work, home, and family life, it's time to move on to the particular items you'll face each day. Yes, we're talking about the dreaded To Do List! Don't run away! The rewards of productivity and peace of mind will greet you on the other side of this chapter!

I have always kept a To Do list of some sort through the years, but it was often on scraps of random paper scattered throughout the house. Those scraps migrated under couch cushions, were laundered with my jeans, and were stuffed into my purse. There was never just one To Do list; there were always several. Determining which items needed to be completed required searching for multiple scraps of paper in some very interesting places.

When my sophisticated –coffee-stained, half-shredded, paper strewn all over the house – system quit working, I realized that I needed a more useful method. I read *Getting Things Done, The Art of Stress-Free Productivity* by David Allen [3], and that book gave me a good foundation for learning how to manage all of my To Do's.

Getting Things Done was very helpful, but it was aimed at a businessman trying to organize his priorities at work. My life is a mix of kids, house, and business so some of David's advice wasn't applicable. I gleaned what information I could from his book, and gradually developed a system that is working for me. In addition to explaining my system, I'll also touch on the To Do list system of several other entrepreneurs. My hope is that by the end of this chapter, you'll have found a system that works for you too.

For those of you who don't use a To Do list, I'm sure your finger is at the ready - about to flip the page and move on to the next chapter. A written To Do list is helpful for everyone; using brain power to constantly cycle, review, and remember a mental To Do list is exhausting and stressful.

According to David Allen, "You should never have the same thought twice, unless you want to." [4] By constantly going over what needs to be done in your head, you are wearing yourself down. By committing those items to a written To Do list, you free up that mental energy to focus on other things. *(I wish I could tell my preschooler not to have the same question twice.... or 1,000 times for that matter! But since I can't, I'll have to settle for organizing my own brain!)*

Having a written To Do list is freeing, not restrictive. With a system that allows you to capture all that needs to be done, you can rest assured that you have not forgotten anything. By putting your list of items to be done on one organized list, you free brain energy to concentrate on the single task at hand.

For my To Do list system, I began by using a plain spiral bound notebook, but now use our specially designed planner, the Brilliant Business Planner, to keep my To Do list.

The notebook or planner is spread open so

that two pages are visible at the same time. The left page is my To Do list, the right page is my weekly schedule.

My To Do list is broken down into a business column and a personal column. I find this separation to be helpful as I tackle each group of items during their designated time of day. At the top of each list I identify my Top 3 Tasks of the week. For other items on the list I will denote with a "C" or a "P" if items on this list need to be done at the computer or the phone. All computer items get done at one time, and all phone calls are done together. This makes for an efficient use of time.

I also separate quick tasks from longer ones. The quick and simple To Do items include phone calls, appointments to be set up, or a quick note to drop in the mail. When I have 5 minutes to kill before I have to do preschool pick-up, I look in one spot to find something useful I can do with those minutes. When these items were jumbled in my long To Do list, they got lost and forgotten too easily.

The To Do list should be comprised of items that need to be done in the near term. Not everything will get done that week, but they are items that need to be completed in the next few weeks.

Below is an example of how I set up the To Do list side of my planner:

Business

MY TOP 3 TASKS:
- Edit next podcast episode
- Reconcile Bank Statement
- Complete Guest Post Article

- take new Etsy photos
- Add new supplies listings to Etsy
- write weekly newsletter email

P - Call printer about quote

C - Send interview requests
C - sign up for CJ
C - pay graphic designer invoice

Personal

MY TOP 3 TASKS:
- Clean bathrooms
- Pay Bills
- Switch out winter clothes

- iron on Girl Scout badges
- research vacation spots

P — Schedule kids well child doctors check-up
P - Call Julie
P - Call Diane, Gretchen, and Christina about play date

C - register kids for summer swim
C - Sign up for kids bowl free
C - purchase teacher gifts

You can head to BrilliantBusinessMoms.com/TMM to grab your own blank copy to use.

I also use my planner to map out my weekly schedule. You may recall from the chapter on time blocking that I loosely divide my days with mornings focused on things at home, afternoons focused on business pursuits, and evenings reserved for dinner, kids' activities, and family time.

Under each day, in keeping with my rough time blocking, I list the home items and business items I plan to tackle that day at roughly the time of day I think they will be tackled. For instance, on Monday morning I may clean the bathrooms and pay bills, and in the afternoon I'll package Etsy orders. Tuesday I might go to the grocery store in the morning and edit a podcast episode in the afternoon. If I finish up the designated task early and have some extra time, I refer to my To Do list for what to tackle next *(or maybe I'll just make some coffee and read a chapter in a book as a reward for working quickly!)*.

At the top of each day I'll write what I plan to make for dinner. *(Something really yummy of course!)*

On the following page is an example of how I transfer my To Do List to different time-blocks throughout the week:

MONDAY	TUESDAY	WEDNESDAY	THURSDAY	FRIDAY	SATURDAY	SUNDAY
JUN 29	JUN 30	JUL 01	JUL 02	JUL 03	JUL 04	JUL 05

Time	MONDAY	TUESDAY	WEDNESDAY	THURSDAY	FRIDAY	SATURDAY	SUNDAY
5							
6							
7							
8							
9	-Edit Podcast Episode	Grocery Store	Clean bathrooms	Target	Laundry	Switch out winter clothes	
10							
11							
12							
1	-Edit Podcast Episode	-Reconcile Bank Statement -Work on guest post	-Finish guest post -Write email	-Take Etsy Photos and Create Listings			
2							
3							
4							
5							
6	Girl Scouts -bring permission slip		Dance -bring Check	Soccer -we are driving Carpool			
7							
8							
9							

This year my schedule is broken up with one child in school all day, one in kindergarten, and one in preschool. The general time blocking concept, and pulling from my To Do list during free minutes has worked for me because I don't have an entire day to systematically go down a list and cross things off. I always have at least one child at home with me. The constant starting and stopping required to get children to school at different times plus evening activities for the kids makes productivity a challenge. Remembering the needs of five people and their activities would be overwhelming without a centralized list!

In addition to my personal To Do list, we use a family calendar, visible to all, to keep track of events and activities.

Make sure all To Do list items are captured. If only half of your To Do list is written down, your mind will still be jumbled with the items not on the list. When you look at your To Do list to make a decision on your next priority, and not every item is captured, some poor decisions will be made. Creating a habit of writing everything on the To Do list is key.

I keep two separate project lists in the back of my planner. One for projects I would like to begin tackling someday, the other for big projects I am currently working on. When I am working on a big project that requires multiple steps, I only include the next step on my To Do list. When that step is done, then I add the next step to my list. Beth Anne covers this topic more in Chapter 2 on being specific. Take that list of small, actionable steps for your big project, and add them, one at a time, to your To Do list. By keeping big current and future projects off your To Do list, you keep your To Do list current and actionable.

I also keep my To Do list clutter free by keeping a separate shopping list. I use a white board on the side of the fridge and break it down by grocery store, Target, and the hardware store. I always list returns I need to make as well.

Now that we have tamed the To Do list, what about the sea of paper you are drowning in? Perhaps you are like me and don't have an office to relegate the paper to. My kitchen is my office. While some dudes may have a corner office, I have a corner of the kitchen counter -- PB&J smears and all. A major problem I used to have was that all the paper coming into the house was going into the kitchen and being spread over the counter tops and table. The kids came home from school, unpacked their backpacks, and left papers all over the hall floor. In addition, I always had a stack of papers that I knew I would need soon or would want for quick reference. These papers included coupons, birthday invitations, or school event information. All papers were stacked on the kitchen counter, and the stack never disappeared. Cooking in the kitchen? Only if you can find a countertop under all the paperwork!

After reading *Getting Things Done*, [3] the first thing I did was set up one centralized inbox. All papers that come in the house go into my pretty wooden inbox purchased from Target: mail, kid's school papers, and all. This box sits on my kitchen counter, but since everything is in the box, the countertops and table stay clean.

Inbox? Check. Now what to do about that other stack of papers I know I will need in the near term? For this I bought a small pretty file box which stores papers I want to quickly retrieve. I'll call this my quick reference file. Nothing stays in the quick reference file for long.

My quick reference file contains a folder for each child, a coupon file, a receipt file, and a near-term file to name a few. If I need to save a birthday invitation so I have the address on the day of the party, it goes in my quick reference file. Preschool payment coupons, the school absence form, Target receipts, the list of classmates, and many more items go in this short term quick reference file box. Items like this used to just sit in a pile on my counter until needed, but now they go in my quick reference file box. This one change in paper management has made a huge difference. Everything is at the tip of my fingers, but not on my countertop. I tuck this file box in a kitchen cabinet.

At the end of every day, I wade through the inbox with my trusty To Do list, file box, and garbage can in tow. I go through every piece of paper in the inbox. A lot of the paper is trash and can be immediately tossed while some papers in the inbox require a small amount of time to handle appropriately. By the time I'm done going through the inbox, it should be empty.

When I go through my inbox, I run across To Do list items. If an item can be done in less than 10 minutes, I tackle it then and there. I don't want a lot of 10 minute tasks cluttering my To Do list. An example of a 10 minute or less task might include responding to an invitation or quickly signing the kids up for soccer online. Some items in my inbox need to be added to the family calendar. Other items may require action taking more than 10 minutes; these are added to the To Do list.

Organizing experts always recommend a filing cabinet for long-term filing of items such as paid bills, mortgage statements, etc. Sorry, not in my stylish kitchen! Is it just me, or does it seem like most items filed away are never needed? Why waste my time filing paperwork I will most likely never need? On the flip side, I'm not quite ready to immediately toss paid utility bills and other items. Maybe I should, but I'm not there yet. My new unorthodox system, which would never be endorsed by productivity experts, is two bins. One bin is for papers I will probably "never-need", but which I can't make myself toss until at least a little time has passed. This includes items such as paid utility bills or credit card statements that I want to keep for at least a little bit. The other bin is for papers I think I "will-need", and might actually need to permanently file at some point. When my husband Mike says, "I'm working on the rental property books, where can I find the paid bills and statements?" I point to the "will-need" bin and all papers he needed were in the bin. Occasionally I take a quick look through the "never-need" bin, and toss most of the papers. When the "will-need" bin gets full, I can choose to permanently file the records I need to keep. That's my system. It's quick, feels safe, and is accessible. Plus permanently filing many papers at one time is more efficient than filing a few pages at a time. These bins can be tucked out of the way to eliminate the eye sore of paper clutter.

If you are interested in going paperless, (a great solution in today's day and age!) my brother Donnie wrote a great book about this topic. You can find it at donnielaw.com/paperless.

When you have completed processing paper in the inbox, it should be empty. You have tossed the paper, completed the item, written it on the calendar, written it on your To Do list, filed it in the quick reference file, or relegated it to a bin. Nothing remains in the inbox. My method of keeping a To Do list may not be your cup of pumpkin-spiced latte and that's fine! Experiment and develop a system that works for you. For me, an empty inbox is a beautiful thing!

Here are some other To Do List methods you might find appealing:

Katie Clemons of Gadanke.com uses an excel spreadsheet to track her various projects and the next action steps required to complete each one. With a young son, Katie often finds she needs to make good use of 10-minute chunks of time. When she gets a free moment, she heads straight to her spreadsheet and tackles the next item on her list. As she explains, if she didn't have a list, she could easily waste those 10 minutes just wondering what she should do next. [5]

There are certainly advantages to an electronic To-Do list, however I would be tempted to add an item to my list and also check email. Guarding against distractions and the rabbit hole of email and social media are key for any electronic To Do list system.

Pat Flynn from the Smart Passive Income Podcast shared in Episode 12 [6] that he uses a folder system to keep track of all the tasks for his various projects. Each project has a designated folder and To Do list. He works on one project with a singular focus until it is done, or until he reaches a stopping point. Then Pat moves on to a different project in another folder. Even though he often has several ongoing projects, a singular focus on one project at a time allows him to accomplish a great deal in his business.

Kelly Meyer from HoleySocksArt.com uses a four quadrant system. The first quadrant in the upper left is for items that are important and urgent. These are must do items! Each day she uses a sticky note and writes down those items and places the note in the first quadrant. The next quadrant is for items that are important, but not urgent. These are items on your To Do list that you want to accomplish, but they haven't reached critical level. Work on these items next. Kelly puts a sticky note on this section too.

The lower quadrants are first comprised of urgent but not important. These are distractions! Answering the telephone just because it rings or answering an email just because it came in are urgent but not important items. Don't get sidetracked on these items when you are working on truly important things.

The last quadrant in the lower right is not urgent and not important. These are time wasters that should be avoided.

Each day Kelly uses her sticky notes to add new tasks to her quadrants. The quadrants help her to stay focused on her main goals for the day and remind her not to be distracted by the urgent items or time wasters.

Here are some other To Do List Ideas from the Brilliant Business Moms Community:

Julie Fuller of TokyoBlossom.Etsy.com says: "I started something new this year, because I didn't want to repeat the overwhelmed feeling I got over the last few months of 2014. I printed off a schedule planner I liked for 2015, put it in a binder and started using that as a 'control center' for everything from when to send in craft show applications to organizing topics for my blog so that I wouldn't attempt to do everything spontaneously this year. I put a few pieces of notebook paper in the back to brainstorm and scribble down ideas."

Marianne Manthey of DesignYourOwnBlog.com uses Asana to schedule tasks for bigger projects and blog posts.

Shaunta Grimes Alburger of GoingReno.com says: "I use a Bullet Journal--just a 97 cent composition book with grid paper from Wal-Mart. I love it to pieces. I actually use two of them--one for my daily to-do list and one for everything else. I use a pants hanger to keep my notebook open with my daily to-do items so it's a constant reminder to me and keeps me on track."

Brooke Sellmann of SillyMamaQuilts.com says, "I have a big white board in my studio. I write ideas on post-it notes and stick them on the board. I have different headings on the board such as urgent, today, and not today to categorize them. Some stick around and others don't....it was a great idea I gleaned from Amanda of TheQuiltedFishPatterns.com."

Is your mind numb from constantly thinking of all you have to do? Experiment with various To Do list systems, and find out what works for you.

The most important things is to have a system with To Do's in one centralized, logical location.

Take-Aways

- It's critical to have a To Do List that works for you.
- Your To Do list should capture every item that needs completed, freeing your mental energy for more important things.
- Experiment with different methods until you find a system that works for you, then work your system.

Chapter 5: Nurturing a New Baby and a New Business -Sarah

You found it! Inspiration for your business or blog idea has finally struck! It solves a problem, there's a clear market for it, and you're passionate about it. You're ready to get to work. But what if this bolt of inspiration happens to coincide with a new baby? I can't think of two more exhausting things: having a brand new baby with all of their needs, and having a business dream you feel you must follow. As a mom you want to be able to savor time with your children without feeling overwhelmed and cranky. Yet you want to be able to satisfy your overwhelming desire to fuel your passions.

A key factor in making all of this work is adjusting expectations. Did you have visions of hand-knitting all of your baby's booties and pureeing all her baby food from organic vegetables that you grew in your backyard? Did you plan for 250 blog posts in the first 6 months of your business formation? Both parenthood and business expectations may need to be adjusted if you are going to keep a smile on your face and hair on your head! The need to focus on only the most important things is going to be even more crucial if you are juggling a baby and a business.

Another expectation that may need to be adjusted is the speed at which you think you can grow your business. Take a minute and breathe. Your business will grow, but not overnight. You are not behind. Set reasonable goals for this time in your life. Unrealistic expectations will leave you feeling frazzled, and maybe even discouraged enough to completely give up. As Kristen from TheFrugalGirl.com says, "Blogging is like a slow-cooker." [7] That sage advice applies to all businesses.

Perhaps you feel the way I do about family. Family is a higher priority than my business. Take time to enjoy that precious, irreplaceable family of yours. Your business will not explode overnight. Set a slow and steady pace and keep on climbing. There is no need to feel like you have to a move a mountain while carrying a baby all in the first week home from the hospital.

Most new moms experience the feeling that they can't seem to get anything done. I know I felt exactly the same way. I discovered that it was not possible to get things done in the way I had before. Before my first baby came along, my time was my own. Life was still busy working a traditional 9-5 job with a long commute, but when I came home, the time was mine. I had large chunks of it to use as I saw fit, plus weekends. I think the biggest adjustment to having children is giving up the freedom you have with your time. Babies need you on their time schedule, not yours.

In this current season of your life, long chunks of focused, uninterrupted time are hard to come by. You need to snatch every spare minute you can and put it to use. You don't have the luxury of only waiting until the baby is napping before you try to get anything done around the house or for your business.

So what does this look like practically? Before babies I could clean the bathrooms all at one time and move on to the next task. After babies it was a little bit at a time. Clean the tub, play with the baby, wipe down the sink, and then feed the baby. After babies, your schedule will look more like this: spend 30 minutes on a blog post, tend to the baby, spend 5 minutes on the business Facebook page, feed the baby, vacuum the family room, and then take the baby for a walk. Even though your time is extremely cut up and choppy, there are small nuggets, or miniscule nuggets, of time available to get things done.

Before babies I could spend all day Saturday working on a business project or idea. My husband Mike and I tried to flip a house before we had babies – for months, every Saturday was devoted to working on the house. *(When we were done, we put the house up for sale, found out I was pregnant a few weeks later, and promptly moved in!)*

The best way to take advantage of these small nuggets of time is to have a plan. In Chapter 4, we discussed different forms and variations of the To-Do list, but the important thing is to **have one.** Maybe your goal each day is just to tackle your #1 most important task! Intersperse your main goal with quick tasks than can fit into those small nuggets of time. If you have those quick tasks on your To Do list, you are much more likely to actually do them when a free moment arises.

When naptime comes, begin tackling the biggest project on your list. Your baby may sleep two hours or 30 minutes, you can never tell. The length of the naptime won't matter if you approach every naptime with hard work and focus on the #1 most important task on your list.

I'm not suggesting that your new life should be all work and no rest. You're a new mom. You're exhausted most of the time. Adjusting to another person's constant needs and the weight of the responsibility can feel overwhelming. Use a couple of the small breaks you get to sit down and relax. Drink a cup of coffee while you read a chapter from a book. Close your eyes and be still for a few moments. Watch a short episode of your favorite comedy on Netflix. You need breaks. But if you're serious about growing a business or accomplishing a big goal, you can't have never-ending breaks. Use breaks to balance concentrated work.

Be mindful of how you spend your precious minutes. If this is break time, treat it like a true break. If this is work time, work as diligently and as quickly as you can. If this is baby time, give that sweet baby all of your attention. It is hard, but try to avoid the mindless activities that can sap you of energy and leave you feeling like you've accomplished nothing. You know what they are; you don't need me to tell you!

There are some ways to steal big chunks of time for your business. I love how Rachel Coley of Candokiddo.com approached her baby and business situation. First, she is always home for her son's afternoon nap time in order to take advantage of that big chunk of time. Second, she takes advantage of the natural alarm clock she now has -- her son. When he wakes up around 5 am for his second feeding, after he goes back to bed, she stays up to take advantage of that chunk of time. Easy? No. Possible? Yes.

Other moms I know have babies that go to bed really early, maybe even 6 or 7 in the evening. If your creative juices start flowing at night rather than the morning, dive into business work as soon as the baby is in bed as many evenings a week as you can. If possible, ask your husband to do the first feeding of the night right before he goes to bed so that you can keep working uninterrupted. On the nights you aren't working, use that same idea and go to bed early with the baby so you can get many hours of uninterrupted sleep before it's your turn for a feeding.

Asking others for help is another way to find large chunks of time to work on your goals. If you ask; Grandma, Grandpa, Dad, or a close friend might be willing to tend to the baby while you squirrel away in your room, feverishly typing out your first novel.

Another way to grab smaller chunks of time might be to save some of baby's favorite things for when you are ready to get some serious work done. Favorite activities might include a swing, the bouncy seat, a new toy, or a new sensory activity.

You, your baby, family and home are wonderfully unique. As your schedule and home begins to fall into a routine, experiment with different ways of managing your time.

Be encouraged that real moms just like you are starting a business or pursuing their passions with a baby on their hip. Be purposeful, have a plan, and enjoy this unique time in your life when you are nursing both a baby and a business. It won't last forever.

In order to savor her days, my friend Diane takes a few minutes when she crawls into bed to think about something her kids and husband did that day that was special, funny, or memorable. Doing this helps her to appreciate her family and notice the wonderful things happening around her each day. Savor each day!

Take-Aways

- Have realistic expectations for yourself and your business.
- Be mindful of how you spend your precious minutes.
- Experiment with different ways of managing your time such as enlisting help or working an unusual schedule to accommodate your new baby.

Chapter 6: Why Habits aren't Just for Nuns
-Beth Anne

There's a story about Jerry Seinfeld *(no one is sure if it's really true!)* but the story goes something like this: A young, aspiring comedian asked Jerry, "What's the secret to being a great comedian?" Jerry replied, "That's easy. To be a great comedian, you have to write great jokes. If you want to write great jokes, you have to write a **lot** of jokes." Legend has it that Jerry committed to writing jokes every single day until he had done it for years without breaking the chain. [8]

When Jerry was later asked about this story,

he had no idea where it came from! Still, this principle applies to just about any enormous goal you may have. If you want to be a great blogger, you have to write great blog posts. If you want to write great blog posts, you have to write a **lot** of posts. If you want to be a great artist, you have to create great art. If you want to create great art, you have to create a **lot** of art.

Sometimes, you'll have to get really creative to make a habit work for you. When Crystal Paine of MoneySavingMom.com wrote her most recent book, she found that waking up early to write wasn't working. She was too distracted and faced too many interruptions. With an already full schedule, she had to come up with a unique solution to complete the book. Crystal started going to bed early at 9 PM or so, then waking up at midnight and writing and researching from midnight to 4 AM each day. Then, she hopped back in bed to catch several extra hours of sleep before starting her day. While this system might not work for everyone, it worked for Crystal, and with her husband on board to help fill in the gaps, Crystal was able to stick to this habit for several months and complete her book. [9]

Whatever your goal is, chances are, you're going to have to do a **lot** of it in order to achieve something of value. Where does this leave us as busy moms? Not all of us have four hours to practice the flute or write our most heartfelt prose. Most of us do, however, have ten minutes. If ten minutes is all you have to give right now, embrace it. **Start** with ten minutes.

As an aspiring writer who worked on her craft for years before getting published, Caroline Starr Rose (http://carolinestarrrose.com) said that when her boys were young, she had to find little nooks of time to write. Just 10 minutes per day had to be enough during that busy time of her life, because otherwise, she would have gotten too discouraged to keep going. Caroline turned those consistent ten minutes into four book deals. Yes, it took her much longer than someone with no children or other responsibilities, but if she had given up in despair and forfeited those ten minutes, she would have precisely zero book deals at the present. [10]

Don't forfeit your future. Your ten minutes matter. Here's what you can do with them:

Make a commitment to spend ten minutes during the first part of each day *(for me, this means any time in the morning)* working towards your big goal. The beautiful thing is, once you sit down and get started, you'll often get caught up in your work and spend much longer than ten minutes. For some unknown reason today is the day that your baby is happily playing on a blanket, your preschooler is intent on an art project and the older kids are playing a game! Be grateful, whatever the reason, for a little longer than ten minutes.

However, if you told yourself that you'd spend two hours on your big goal at the beginning of each day, the task might feel impossible. You'd be too discouraged to sit down and get started. Set a small, realistic goal, but make it a daily habit.

Nathan Barry shared on his podcast that he'd been mulling over writing a book for quite some time, and he finally committed to writing one thousand words each day. He printed out a calendar with a whole year's worth of days right in front of him. For every day that he wrote one thousand words, he'd put a red X over the day to mark his accomplishment. [11] Carla Patton of ThisMessyHeart.com takes habit-tracking to a new level of fun by giving herself a gold star on each day she completes her habit. Whether it's an X, gold star, or writing out the words, "You did it!" the importance lies in noting your accomplishments and holding yourself accountable to that habit.

Nathan admits that it took him a few attempts to really get a good chain going. At first, he wrote for eight days in a row. Then he made it to fifteen days. After eighty days of writing in a row, Nathan published his App Design Handbook. The day after publishing, his Commit App popped up to ask if he was going to write one thousand words that day. His initial reaction was, no! He'd already written his book and met his goal. Ultimately he decided he wanted to keep the chain going and see what it would turn into. It turned into several more books and writing one thousand words per day for over six hundred days in a row! [11]

We've created a habit tracker for you to use to hold yourself accountable to your goals. You can grab it at BrilliantBusinessMoms.com/TMM On the next page is an example of how I used a habit tracker like this one when I was training for my second half-marathon last summer and fall. *(Unfortunately, I didn't have a lovely design like the one we have now!)* I didn't run every day, but I did track weekly mileage goals and the habit tracker ensured that I made forward progress each week.

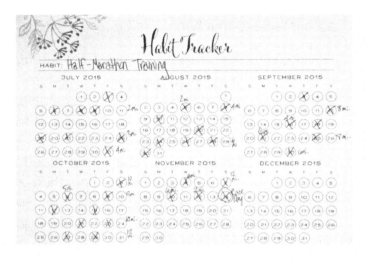

More recently, I've used a similar method to keep me on track with working on the book and planner launch. While my goal wasn't writing 1,000 words per day, because I personally find writing to be much easier than editing or the other important tasks in my business, I did have a goal to do something to move us forward towards the book and planner launch each day.

For me, building a habit of making progress towards my big goal was so key. When I was tempted to get off-track, I'd ask myself, "what am I doing today to propel this project forward?" As someone who struggles with far too many ideas and starting far too many projects at once, holding myself to a daily habit helps me to finish a project and accomplish something of value.

Tracking my habit towards this big goal became even more important as we neared launch day. I have a mental block when it comes to finishing my work and putting it out into the world. But when I saw two or more blank days staring back at me on my habit tracker, it was a powerful reminder to get back to work - to not let my fears keep me from doing what I set out to do.

It's really incredible what a visual reminder of your habit can do for you. Once you get going, you won't want to break your chain. It feels great to be able to say you worked one hundred days in a row towards your big goal. It feels even better to achieve five hundred days!

No matter your goal: running a marathon, starting a non-profit to support a cause you believe in, raising funds to adopt a child, earning a full-time income through your Etsy shop - committing to that goal on a daily basis makes all the difference.

Take-Aways

- As busy moms, you can start chipping away at your big goal with just 10 minutes per day.
- Set a daily habit of working on your big goal
- Use a checklist or calendar to track each day you've spent working on your goal.
- Build up those days to create a chain.
- Don't break the chain! Keep going! You'll be amazed at what you can accomplish over time by making small progress each day.

Chapter 7: Pick a Date, Pick a Person, and Get to it!
-Beth Anne

One of the most important factors in achieving your goals is setting a due date for all of the tasks involved, and finding someone who will hold you accountable. As a serial idea-machine, sticking to one task and holding myself accountable for its completion is incredibly difficult for me.

I'm scared to think about how little I would accomplish if I didn't have others holding me accountable. Even very important tasks such as sending my son Holden's adoption postplacement reports to India on time can be quite difficult for me. The only reason I get them done is because our adoption agency holds me accountable.

In college, I wrote great papers, but without fail, no matter how much I prepared and researched ahead of time, I would still be up until 5 AM the morning the paper was due to polish things off and get the task finished! The due date plus a waiting professor held me accountable to completing the project.

It's rather embarrassing to admit, but even necessary tasks like the ones mentioned above, can get lost in the swirling winds of my idea-ridden brain. Why am I mentioning what a total novice I am as I try to teach **you** how to be more productive? If a novice like me can accomplish big things such as writing a book or creating a planner because someone is holding me accountable, then imagine what you, as an organized, mature person can do!

The two key people most responsible for my ability to get things done are my husband, Chris, and my sister and business partner, Sarah. Maybe for you, it's your best friend, a fellow Etsy seller or a blogging buddy that you met online. The "who" of the matter is not nearly as important as the quality of the relationship and their ability to hold you accountable to your biggest goals.

For example, Chris holds me accountable to my personal goals such as exercising or working with Holden on physical therapy. He kindly, casually, and gently asks me, "What's your workout for today?" or "What's our PT plan going to be for Holden today?" Chris isn't a drill sergeant about it *(surprisingly enough since he's a Marine!)*; he reminds me in a kind, gentle way. There's no enjoyment in nagging, but rather enjoyment in watching me commit and succeed at something. If possible, it's incredibly helpful to have someone who's invested in the project to help with accountability. Chris is just as invested as I am in our son Holden's progression with PT, and so it's easier for him to make sure we stay on track.

For the business, I'm so lucky to have my sister Sarah as an equal partner and someone who's equally invested in our projects. When she checks in on how the book is going, she does so as someone who's devoted to the success of the project *(not as an annoying, know-it-all big-sister! Ok.. maybe every once in a while it feels that way!)*. I know this kind of working relationship may not be possible for everyone, but if it is, seek out those people! Find someone who's interested in business, blogging, writing, Etsy selling, or whatever it is that YOU do because they're immediately more involved in your quest.

Once you've settled on those key people who will hold you accountable, you have to give them clear dates and deadlines for your tasks and goals. Otherwise, they have nothing to truly hold you accountable to - and chances are, they'll be way too nice to tell you to pick up the pace on your book and write 5 more pages each day!

In my personal life, registering for a half-marathon on Day 1 of training turned out to be an excellent decision. Having a due date for my big goal was critical to my success. Not only did I have a due date, I had someone who was invested in the project to hold me accountable for its completion. A friend and military spouse who was an experienced runner felt confident that I could complete a half marathon with 9 weeks of training. She was running the race too and offered to hold me accountable to my training schedule.

Before I signed up for the race, I hadn't gone jogging in over a year. My husband was deployed, and I was balancing life with Holden. The farthest distance I had ever run before was 6 miles, and now I planned to more than double that distance in 9 weeks. After my very first training run of just 2 miles, I posted on my personal Facebook page that I was training for a half-marathon on March 9th. Now, my big goal was out there for the world to see. There was no turning back!

To this day, I can't believe that I trained for that race in 9 weeks and completed it in under a 9 minute per mile pace. If I hadn't committed to a clear deadline for completing the race or someone who was counting on me to run it, I would have wimped out and would probably **still** be training towards my very first half-marathon a year later. The due date kept me on track, even on rough days when running 6 miles with the jogging stroller felt impossible, when I didn't feel like I had the time to run for two hours, or when I had to train in 18-degree weather and snow during a visit home to Pittsburgh.

I don't share this story to suggest that everyone reading this book should sign up and train for a half-marathon in 9 weeks. We each have our own strengths and our own big goals to work towards. Running has always been enjoyable to me, and endurance is one of the very few athletic qualities I possess. If someone had tried to convince this 5'2", uncoordinated lady to sign up for a Volleyball tournament, the answer would have been "No way!" as I sprinted in the other direction!

This same principle of due dates and accountability comes into play for your biggest goals and passions. You'll be amazed at how much more you can get done when you have a due date for completion instead of just throwing up your hands and saying, "Oh well, maybe someday it will happen."

Sarah and I set a very brave due date for our Podcast Launch last year. I called her in early April of 2014 and told her my idea. I wanted to create a podcast just for moms who were working on the side while spending time with their children. Unlike so many of my other crazy ideas, she was immediately excited and saw the value of providing interviews and business content to other moms. We didn't set a due date right away, but we did begin reaching out to potential guests and researching equipment to get started.

A few weeks later after we interviewed our first guest, our sister-in-law Abby Lawson of JustaGirlandHerBlog.com reached out to us to let us know that her first book would be launching on June 10th, 2014, and that if we were uncertain of a Podcast launch date, perhaps that would be a great choice so she could share the episode on her book launch page.

At that point, we knew we had to do it! We still had so many things to figure out such as how to initiate, record, and edit a group Skype call. *(Our first 2 interviews were in person with all 3 people hovering over the same little Snowflake microphone!)* Even though we had so much to figure out, we knew we'd be missing a huge opportunity if we couldn't jump on Abby's promotion train. Being virtually unknown in the online space, other than our Etsy shop, meant we had to work really hard for each new listener.

Once we set our launch date for the podcast, I started telling everyone I knew about it - both online and off. Just like I had done for my half-marathon goal, I put our new goal of launching a podcast out into the world for everyone to see. I knew I had too much pride to not follow through on my word, and Sarah was counting on me too.

When we set this deadline in May, Chris had just come home from deployment 2 weeks earlier. We were about to leave for a 10-day vacation to Spain, and Sarah and her husband Mike were remodeling their kitchen.... themselves! Despite our crazy schedules, we set a deadline and we stuck to it.

Yes, Sarah and I worked our podcasting buns off during that time period. We were down to the wire trouble-shooting Skype-recording and editing software and booking guests to fill out the coming weeks. Every day we were on the phone trying to come up with solutions, ordering equipment, and assigning short tasks for each other to then re-convene the next day.

I remembered hearing Pat Flynn saying that from the time he announced his intentions to start a podcast to when he actually launched it, 18 months had passed! We were determined not to let that happen. We wanted to launch, even though we knew it wouldn't be perfect. We listened to our audience and gradually refined our message and presentation. There are still so many areas of improvement for our podcast, yet every week people tell us how much they appreciate it and how much it has helped them grow their business. Thankfully for them, we didn't wait until the podcast was perfect to launch!

The initial due date and having each other as accountability partners, forced us to push ourselves as never before. It was not a level we could have sustained forever, but for that time, it was necessary and we're so proud that we did it. On the other side of that crazy time, we're thankful for this journey and for all the talented, kind, brilliant women who have become part of our online community.

Even with serious structure and your very best intentions, there will inevitably be life events that are out of your control. When a crisis arises or your family needs extra attention, give yourself grace to push your deadlines back and create a realistic timeline. After all, we're pursuing our passions in the margins of our day, because our families come first.

On the reverse side of things, be careful not to let two days of the sniffles or one night of poor sleep de-rail your entire project. Take the bumps in stride. Keep pushing forward, and only push back those deadlines when it's absolutely necessary for your own health and well-being, and that of your family.

With solid deadlines and someone supportive to hold you accountable, we're confident that you will accomplish more than you ever thought possible.

Take-Aways

- Find the right people who will be kind, encouraging, and supportive, yet honest and   straightforward accountability partners.
- Set firm due dates for yourself.
- Announce your goals publicly to add an extra layer of accountability.
- Don't forget to leave room for grace as a busy mom!

Chapter 8: Why Ideas are Like Sprinkles + How to Save them All! -Beth Anne

As women with plenty of passion and big dreams, we often have big ideas that race right alongside those dreams. What do you do when your next big idea strikes? Do you drop everything and rush to get to work? What about that deadline for tomorrow.... or the great big goal you're currently working on? Do they still matter? Have they become irrelevant in light of your newfound wisdom and understanding? "Yes, this is the **one**!" You're sure of it.

Ideas are the life-blood of an entrepreneur. We encourage them the way we encourage the presence of sprinkles atop those soft sugar cookies from the grocery store. The more the merrier, but the more sprinkles there are, the more those tiny rascals fall off and are lost forever to the germy grave of Walmart's bakery floor.

Don't let your ideas flit away and die like those tiny sprinkles. Just as importantly, don't let your current goals and plans fall by the wayside like giant shoulder pads and big hair! *(C'mon, fess up! I know you had those giant double-bangs floating proudly and stiffly six inches above your head just like I did!)*

We have a solution to help you to continue to care for your current *project (yes, it's going to need a lot of hair-spray and touch-ups!)* while savoring every last sprinkle of that new idea.

You need an idea-catching system.

The system itself is far less important than the fact that you have one.

Sarah Mackenzie of AmongstLovelyThings.com uses a simple black notebook. As a homeschooling mom to 6 kids, she needs something that's easily accessible at any moment throughout her day. She generally keeps the notebook in the kitchen, which is close to the table where school happens. [12]

Sarah admits that her ideas are random and unorganized in the notebook, but it still accomplishes two things:

> 1. She no longer fears forgetting an idea and racking her brain trying to remember it later. *(This is both a time-waster and a total downer if the idea is lost!)*
> 2. She can remain fully present with her kids during the day instead of distractedly turning that idea over in her brain. By focusing on the task at hand, she's more productive.

Occasionally, Sarah says, she goes back through her notebook to remember things that she still wants to try while crossing off other things that now seem not-so-great.

My own idea-catcher of choice is Evernote. Evernote works well for me, because as a mama to just one fairly non-mischievous 4 year-old, it's generally not a big deal to have the laptop easily accessible throughout the day. I limit its use during quality-time with Holden, but since all my ideas end up on the computer, it's easy enough to pop on for 2 minutes, type things out, and move on.

For video tutorials on how to use Evernote to organize not just your ideas, but your entire life, I recommend Donnie Lawson's video course at donnielaw.com/paperless. *(Full disclosure: he's our brother. Fuller disclosure: I'm such a nitpicker I wouldn't dare share my own brother's work unless it was pretty awesome.)*

Here's how I use Evernote:

1. I create folders for the topics that I learn about most often or for those that I have the most ideas. Two examples would be Pinterest strategies and tips, or book ideas. I also have a general business ideas folder which I use for any new product idea that we may develop in the future - whether it be for our Etsy shop or our blog.
2. I create a new note for each new idea.
3. I tag each note with relevant keywords so I can easily search for it and find it later. Don't obsess over this step. 2 tags are generally plenty for me. Example: book idea; productivity
4. I type out my idea as fast as I can. As long as I can understand it, I don't bother to correct spelling mistakes.

Speed and stream of consciousness are important.

5. I move on. I don't let myself continue to mull the idea over forever and forsake my current, less exciting projects. After all, I sat down and planned out my year, my month, and my week, and decided that my current project was really important when it came to reaching my biggest goals.

Don't let one new idea, or ten new ideas, for that matter, de-rail your most important project. Jumping on each new idea that comes our way is the entrepreneur's highest form of self-sabotage. I absolutely understand the allure of abandoning a current project's difficulties for a shiny new project. It's scary to finish a product and put ourselves out there. What if we missed the mark? What if everyone hates it? The perfectionist in us is scared to death of even one person who doesn't like what we do. We create nightmare scenarios that keep us up at night. **For the record: there will probably be someone who hates what you do. Do it anyway.**

The only way you'll ever get feedback, learn, refine, and get better is by putting yourself out there. You're exactly right to feel nervous or scared, but as Henry Ford says, "Whether you think you can or you can't, you're right." *(Just so you know, We think you can!)* You may have ten products that fail, but you'll never know if you keep chasing every new whim that enters your brain. You may have one product that's a huge success, but you'll never know unless you put it out there.

Catching your ideas and saving them for later is key to being a focused and productive goal-getter and mom.

What if You Just Can't Get That Idea off of Your Mind?

When you're just too excited about your ideas not to share them, call a friend, your business partner, your mom, or just bombard your spouse with your ideas at the end of a long day!

It's wonderful to get almost-immediate feedback on whether your crazy new idea has any merit or not. For me, it's one more cathartic step that helps me to **release the idea and return to my current projects.**

Now, if you happen to be my spouse, or my

sister **and** my business partner, you may find my habit of idea-dumping to be a bit cumbersome. I'm very sorry. I have no words of wisdom for you. My recommendation is to dump your thoughts and feelings on someone else. My brain is too full of ideas to handle it!

Just-In-Time Learning

While we're talking about overloaded brains, let's discuss the sheer volume of information available on growing a business. Even though it's tempting, I know I can't spend all day just reading books, blog posts, and absorbing information on growing our business. I'd never have a business to grow if I did this!

Instead, I use a technique called Just-in-Time Learning. I learned about it from Pat Flynn. *(In case you haven't noticed - we're big fans of his!)* The internet and a few tools make this strategy so easy to implement.

When you run across a fabulous article or resource that you may need later, just bookmark it in Evernote and move on. When you're ready to tackle the beast that is Twitter, write that novel or take photos that are finally better than your two year-old's, your resources will be catalogued and waiting for you.

Pinterest is another great way to sort your favorite resources on the web. Again, you'll probably have to do a quick skim of the article to see if there's any value there, but the second you know there **is** value, and it's simply not the time to spend an hour learning headline hacks, Pin that gem and move on.

When all else fails, there's a good chance that the all-mighty, mostly-benevolent Googlebots will help you find anything you're looking for when you need it.

Information-overload is often another strategy for putting off the most important tasks that need to be done. It feels so good and noble because you're learning, and sure, one day you might actually use all of that knowledge. But trust me, if you create a bad habit of learning at the expense of doing, you'll be loads smarter and have the perfect invisible clothing line, inaudible podcast, and untouchable vase. Bummer.

Ideas are awesome. As entrepreneurs, we love them! Ideas keep us excited about our business plans, allow us to create new things, and help us work in new ways. Without a plan and focus to reign them in, you'll just chase them haphazardly around the grocery store trying to savor what's left of that dirty, germ-infested sprinkle. Don't despair, with an idea-catching system in place, you can confidently ask for more sprinkles, please!

Our Brilliant Business Moms' Community has several other great strategies for idea catching:

Helen Xia of HelenHandmade.com loves Evernote too: "I use Evernote to keep track of ideas, photos of inspiration, goals, to-do lists, and even business receipts. The mobile app really allows me to brain dump on the go. But I also use Google Drive to keep more extensive project ideas, like an editorial calendar, product list, project planner, etc. I love both tools because you can access them just about anywhere at any time, even without Internet access."

Cheri Tracy of Orglamix.com says, "I use an app called Anote. It's really simple yet colorful and easily customizable. It allows me to categorize and tag everything as well as set up reminders and goals. I brain dump everything in here. Then I print them out each Sunday and organize them by priority. It keeps me focused. "

Ashley Monda of OurFullTable.com says, "For my blog I just make a draft in Wordpress with the title as the idea. That way if I need a post I can refer to all my drafts. If it's for my Business I write it in my planner in a specific spot. Then I can scroll back thru when I need motivation. If those methods are not available right away I use the notes section in my iPhone. "

Tammy Haskett-Anderson of SpeckledOwls.Etsy.com says, "I keep a notebook in my purse to jot ideas down while I'm out and about. On my work bench, I cover it with white contact paper so while I am working I have a quick place to jot it down right there on my bench. I transfer all of my notes into an "idea notebook" and start with a new sheet of contact paper about once a month. If I'm really having a creative moment while laying in bed I use my phone and just speak my idea into it and it goes right into my notes."

Cortney Nichols of DownJoyfulLane.Etsy.com says: "I keep a yearly calendar (a big one that I can see all at once) and spread out my ideas. For example if I wanted to start a podcast, I would pick a month and put that idea on that month. Now the idea is out of my head and I don't have to think about until then."

Take-Aways

- Ideas are a necessary part of being an entrepreneur
- Develop an idea-catching system so you can stay focused on your current project and address those great ideas at the right time.
- Use just-in-time learning to make sure you don't succumb to information-overload.
- Catalog and share your ideas so you can get back to work on your big project.

Chapter 9: "No" Can be a Positive Word
-Beth Anne

Women are so good at saying yes. We grew up hearing that being helpful and putting others' needs before our own is virtue of the highest order. If you don't volunteer for something, it might not get done. If not you, then who? Saying no often makes us feel guilty or uncomfortable while saying yes makes us feel great.

When someone needs a meal, a babysitter, a volunteer, snacks for the class, a chaperone, or even a chauffeur, we're on it! Every time we say yes without thoughtfully considering what that "yes" means, we are saying no to something else. Our goals, dreams, and the very best God has for us may be chipped away by that little "yes".

We give pieces of ourselves to others day in and day out. Some of those pieces are rightfully given – to our spouses, our children, our dearest friends and family, and others that we feel called to serve. Some of those pieces are given begrudgingly, because we were pressured, or felt guilty, or no one else said yes. A begrudging, guilty "yes" is often worse than an honest "no."

While we grumpily go through the motions of an act of service or commitment that we don't really want to do, our family receives the brunt of our discontent. They hear our moaning. They see our tired bodies. They get our seconds while we plaster on a sugary smile and hand over the casserole.

This year, one of my commitments is to make sure that my family gets my very best. I want to serve others too, but I'm walking on shaky ground when that serving demotes my family to last place.

This truth is really hard to accept: It's not our job to fix everyone else's life. I love to help others. *(Chances are, you do too!)* I love to encourage. When others are struggling, I want to be their go-to girl. Not every difficult situation or problem is mine to fix. It is my responsibility to carefully consider where I'm being called to serve and give, and to have the courage to say no to those things that aren't part of that calling.

There are times of crisis when we need to drop everything and help others. I am wholeheartedly for a "yes" like that. But sometimes it feels as though someone else's lack of planning becomes our crisis. We must master the art of saying no.

When we completed the 25 Things exercise in chapter 1, we decided what was most important to us this year. In doing so, we also decided what was not as important. Our priorities and commitments may change from year to year, but if we don't protect our highest goals and values with fervor, they could get trampled on by the goals and priorities of others.

As a Christian, I've decided that the only influences on how I spend my time are God, my spouse, and my family. I make my decisions prayerfully with this in mind. If you're a Christian too, I'm confident that when God wants you to step up and serve those around you, He'll make it really clear. If you're not a Christian *(and even for those who are!)* consider the top five passions you outlined at the beginning of the book. Let those guide you as you make crucial choices about how to spend your time.

The other beautiful thing about picking our highest passions and focusing on those is that it gives us breathing room in our day. When a friend truly does need our help, we can easily reach out and offer a rested, steady hand. When a new ministry opportunity becomes available, we may find that we have a few hours per week to devote to it.

Confession Time: I haven't always been the best at saying "no". In college, it's hard to even recall all of the different ministries, honor society positions, research projects, and other activities I committed to. There are so many little yes's that I regret. Who knows who may have stepped up in my place and been an absolute blessing to others in a position that truly was a calling for them? My less-than-best yes's, meant giving far less than my best in each position. I regret my attitude, my lack of focus, and my inability to make a meaningful difference because I was torn in so many different directions. Often I traded genuine relationships for a few extra bullet points on my resume or anecdotes to include in cover letters. Wow, that really stings, and it's something I'm still working on today.

On the reverse side of things, I don't believe you'll regret the times when you earnestly consider and pray over an opportunity to serve or a calling and move forward with confidence in the **best** choice for your life. **Yes** a million times over to those things!

I wish I could tell you that my story ended there -- that from college onwards I've said yes to nothing but the best for me and my family. For some reason, my husband Chris' first deployment seemed to turn "no" into a forbidden word again. Many spouses, with a full resume of past deployment experience advised me: "You need to keep busy. Put your focus on others' and you won't think so much about yourself or how lonely you are."

I listened naïvely. I'd never done this before and though their advice raised a few doubts in my mind, what did I know?   They were older and wiser. If I had simply taken the advice that I've now carefully written in this book, I wouldn't be embarrassed as I share what happened next.

Holden had two surgeries and far too many

doctor appointments, tests, and procedures to count in his first seven months at home. Chris left for deployment after just three months as a new dad. At two and a half years old, Holden needed time and space to adjust to a brand new life in a completely different country, learning a completely different language, and learning to trust us as mom and dad.

I naively volunteered for the children's ministry at church, offered our house as a host home for a small group Bible study, signed up for cooking club, picked up night shifts as a nurse, and Sarah and I decided to start a mommy blog! Oh boy! I'm confident that you're much wiser than me.

It's probably no surprise that I flaked out on being a host home two months into the study. There's a key detail about small group that I should probably mention: Holden was often a crying mess upstairs in the playroom with the sitter while we tried to have Bible Study downstairs. I wish I would have taken the hint sooner that the whole thing was just too much for him at the time. I regret not paying more attention to what he needed. I put the opinions of others before the needs of my own child. That's not ok.

After months of flaky attendance as a children's ministry volunteer, I finally resigned that role too. Towards the end, I felt that I was not nearly as kind and patient with the kids as I should have been, and I was so tired of feeling like I let everyone down each week. This is a role I would love to do again, but after prayerfully considering it, this year is not the year.

Finally, just before Chris returned from a nine-month deployment, I wised up and cleared my schedule to focus on my family. I will always regret putting the opinions and thoughts of others before what I knew was best for my family, but I'm thankful for the lessons I learned during that time. I'm so much more thoughtful and prayerful before I commit to something these days.

On the other hand, with a much more open schedule, I feel thankful for the ability to embrace the sacred moments God places in front of me. When I'm called to something, it's easy enough to drop everything and follow that call. My hope for you is that by learning that art of saying "no", saying yes to those acts of service where you clearly feel God's call on your heart will be so much easier.

Why is Saying No So Difficult?

Saying "no" sounds like the perfect solution to our overflowing schedules, but in practice, it can be **so difficult**. Why is this?

We often worry about several things when we say no.

- I'm concerned about what others will think of me.
- I'm letting others down.
- I'm missing out on an opportunity
- I want to be agreeable

What Will People Think?

There are very few individuals' opinions on this earth that should really matter to us. For me, it's God's, my spouse's, my family, and my closest friends. As women, we're so easily lured into the trap of pleasing others, even if it shouldn't make one bit of different whether that other person feels pleased with us or not. Of course we don't want to be rude simply because we don't care what someone thinks, but on the other hand, we shouldn't allow an acquaintance to take their red pen and fill up our schedule.

If you say no tactfully, most people will

consider you a thoughtful person. You're not a flake who over-commits and then fails to deliver. Over-commitment is a crummy feeling. You're scattered, stressed, and chances are, not very fun to be around either! When you fail to meet your commitments, the people who were counting on you feel pretty crummy too!

If for some reason someone's opinion of you was changed because of one *(or maybe a few)* "no's", then they're probably not someone with whom a long-term relationship makes sense. The people who matter most will understand and appreciate your thoughtful "no".

Letting Others Down

Although this is closely tied to letting go of what others' think, some of us are so incredibly helpful that the thought of letting someone down is almost too much to bear! But in many cases, by saying "yes", you may be letting down those people who are most important to you in favor of not letting down a casual acquaintance. When the calling is there, that's completely different. But when you don't feel called, don't let someone else's potential disappointment stop you from making the right choice.

Missing Out on an Opportunity

You've already decided what your most important goals are for the year. You're committed to getting things done and creating the right opportunities for yourself. If this "ask" truly falls within your big goals for the year, then by all means, say "yes!" Hopefully, you've left plenty of room in your schedule to seize a great opportunity when it comes along!

Kelly Meyer of HoleySocksArt.com says, "If it's something I'm interested in but just can't take the time right now, then I like to say, "Unfortunately I can't right now, but I hope to be more free in ___. Please feel free to reach out to me then." Sometimes great opportunities just need different timing and a window left open."

If it's an opportunity that sounds great for another year but is not in line with your highest priorities this year, then you need to trust the process. Believe that when you're ready, opportunities in this particular area will still abound.

I Want to be Agreeable

This trait of agreeableness in women – it's a beautiful thing. We enjoy working on teams and cooperating from a young age. I fondly remember creating new games and acting out elaborate scenarios with my childhood friends and our dolls. We're wired for community. Often, we get more done and accomplish bigger tasks because we're so adept at working together.

However, this same trait can work against us when our priorities don't line up with others. Smiling, offering feigned enthusiasm, and saying "yes" to every little thing can sometimes feel like a membership requirement for the female race.

Did you know that you can say "no" with a smile too? It's possible to say "no" in an agreeable, pleasant way that acknowledges the importance of the request as well as the value of the person asking. "No" doesn't need to be rude, off-putting, or alienating. You can continue to be agreeable and be part of a group while giving a thoughtful no.

I love Victoria Wilson of VictoriaEasterWilson.com's strategy for giving a pleasant "no": Your *(thing)* sounds so fun. I wish I could commit, but I can't. *(This resource)* may help you with *(planning/telling others)*. Good luck."

Strategies for Giving a Thoughtful "No"

Now that we've broken down all of the

negative connotations associated with "no", we're still left with the courageous act of actually using it. How can we be armed and ready at that critical moment instead of sheepishly calling to cancel a week later?

I am so guilty of this. My guts vanish when the moment comes. Saying "no" is something that still requires practice and exercise for me. The ideas below help me to be ready with just the right response instead of wimping out.

One of my favorite responses comes from Lysa TerKeurst's book, *The Best Yes*.

"I'm sorry, but right now, I cannot give this project the time and attention that it deserves." [13]

Our Brilliant Business Moms Community had several other great ideas for giving a thoughtful no:

- I'm not the best person to help on this.
- Right now is not a good time for me.
- I'd love to do this but....
- Let me think about this and get back to you.
- "It's just a "no" for today." *(This one comes from one of the kindest nurses I've ever*

worked with. She uses it both at work and at home with her kids!)

- Julie Fain of TagandTibby.com: "I give parameters. For example at my children's school I told them I can volunteer on Thursdays, but only on Thursdays.
- "Dana Regehr of JanieLaneStudio.Etsy.com "Let me ask my husband about that first." Such wise advice because I think I can do it all! He is wonderful at truly helping me sort through the schedule and understanding my capacity and that of my family. I might be able to do it, but my boys may struggle if I do it. It puts us on the same page and we work better as a team. Plus, when I go back and tell someone that we have talked about it and it's not a good time for our family, they have a harder time insisting that I commit."

These are all great responses! I know there's one that will work for you.

As we journey on the road to making the next twelve months full of intention and the very best, I hope we will say goodbye to the easy "yes" and the overwhelm that comes with it. You can do it, and I promise we'll still love and respect you after you give us a thoughtful "no."

Take-Aways

- Saying "no" is necessary in order to give our most important passions and priorities our full attention and focus.
- Saying "no" is difficult because we worry about what others will think and don't want to let anyone down.
- There are many great strategies for saying no that will help you to be prepared to give the right answer.

Chapter 10: Sleep: How you Can Get More of It & Still Get More Done!
-Beth Anne

Let me start this chapter with a Disclaimer: If you're a mom to a newborn, or any child who struggles with sleep each night, I sincerely apologize! This chapter is not for you. Shield your eyes! Reading about how a lack of sleep can affect your health and well-being is the **last** thing you need to hear right now. What you need to hear is that "this too, shall pass." Someday, your little ones will sleep again, and when they do, we hope you'll commit to getting more sleep too.

Until then, keep pressing onward, keep pushing through those foggy, blurry days, because that's the best you can do. We're here for you.

In Chapter 9, we talked about saying no to those things that are less than the best for you right now. Saying yes to your best isn't just about your calendar, it involves taking care of your body too. My old go-to for getting more done and cheating the system was to get less sleep. No more! I promise you that chronic sleep deprivation is not the best of what the world has for you. Did you know that you can be more productive when you spend less time working and get more sleep?

Here's a picture of what my sleep-deprived life used to look like: "No big deal," I thought as I looked at the clock, "I'm planning to stay up all night anyways...." It was 10 PM already, and I had hours of work ahead of me to get ready for our podcast launch the next day.

I obsessed over show notes and cover photos, playing with 50 different fonts and formats for hours. I edited and re-edited the page - wanting each line to be perfect, but knowing **with each passing hour that my brain was less and less able to do its best work.**

All-nighters were a recurring theme in my life since high school. I loved the feeling of stealing time – of getting more out of each day than anyone else I knew. I was cheating the system, and it felt great!

The Slippery Slope

My first all-nighter happened out of necessity. I had an important paper to write for AP English, and because of other tests, volunteering, tennis, and college applications that week, I had to complete the entire paper in one night. Never one to submit less than my best work, I stayed up all night reading, researching, and crafting my thesis.

The next morning, I got in the shower as usual, put on a little extra under-eye concealer, and headed off to high school in a daze. Amazingly, I was able to stay awake and *(I thought)* pay attention in all my classes. I didn't even need caffeine to stay up all night or to stay awake the next day! My friends looked at me wide-eyed when I told them what I'd done. Most of them wandered through their day like zombies too, and that was with six or seven hours of sleep. My paper earned an A, and all of a sudden, a whole new world was opened up to me.

Maybe I didn't need as much sleep as the average person. I had a secret super power, and from that point on, I intended to use it as much as possible. Throughout my senior year of high school, college, and my early working years, I lived by these lines from Edna St. Vincent Millay:

"My candle burns at both ends;
It will not last the night;
But ah, my foes, and oh, my friends—
It gives a lovely light!"

"Sleep is for unmotivated losers," I sincerely thought. "Who cares if my life-expectancy is shortened a bit, I'm going to **live** – really **live**." I mistakenly thought there was something noble about railing against the body's most rational needs and beating the humanity out of myself.

In college, I routinely studied for Organic Chemistry and Calc III by staying up all night then strolling into the classroom to problem-solve my way through the tests like any other student. Surprisingly, I did well. At the time, I was smugly oblivious to all of the downsides of my lifestyle.

When I finally settled on a career in nursing, I knew the night shift would be perfect for me. I was one of the few RNs on the floor still peppy and smiling after a twelve-hour shift. By this time, I'd discovered the miracle nectars of coffee and Red Bull. I drank both in large quantities every night. My co-workers shook their heads in dismay. The residents wondered what in the world there was to smile about at six AM on a Saturday!

Lack of Focus

What I later realized was that I wasn't cheating any system except my own body's. After an all-nighter, my brain felt foggy. "What was I working on? What am I supposed to do today?" were frequent questions floating lazily in my mind. I couldn't focus, and even more importantly, I couldn't even prioritize simple tasks and figure out where to start. After an all-nighter or a three-hour night, I would look back on the day and wonder what I had gotten done. "Where did all those hours go?" I honestly couldn't even remember.

Science backs up my experience of the sleep-deprived, brain-haze. One study of 17 subjects showed that just 24 hours of sleep deprivation caused their entire brains to be less active – with even larger decreases in activity in the areas that control alertness, attention, and higher-order cognitive processes. As the markers for brain activity decreased, both alertness and cognitive performance decreased in the test subjects. [14] Makes sense, right?

Increased Anxiety

Something strange started happening during those all-nighters too. My mind would enter into this frantic state. My already too-full brain would flood with hundreds more ideas. It felt like a sandstorm attacking every neuron.

As a new entrepreneur trying to grow a podcast, blog, and Etsy Shop, ideas on new products, topics to write about, and ways to market the business became overwhelming. With so many of them taking over my every thought, I couldn't focus. I couldn't find a way to block them out and get started on anything. As a result, I felt anxious much of the time. Imagine trying to build a sand castle in that perpetual sandstorm. I was so busy just trying to protect myself from the battering that building anything of value seemed like an impossible feat. Many studies show that subjects report an increase in anxiety after sleep deprivation. [15]

Poor Mood

Outside of my own mind, my relationships

with others began to suffer. I know for sure that I caused stress for my sister and business partner. There was always something urgent we needed to do right that very second to grow our business. These directives were announced in panicked, caffeine-driven states. By the next day, there would be five new things we needed to do, and the list from yesterday seemed completely irrelevant and trivial.

After I became a mom, and every fiber of patience and understanding was tested on a daily basis, I realized with great clarity how important sleep was to my relationships. I was more likely to get emotional or irritated over minor things when it came to my preschooler. "Am I seriously crying right now because his shirt is too short and we need to find another one to wear? What is going on?"

I could see the confused look in my son's eyes too. "I mean, there are really important things to be upset about like running out of chocolate chips or not getting the ninja turtle cup, but this mom?.... This?" There are, embarrassingly enough, 50 other options in his closet. Literally, I could walk ten steps, problem solved.

A study of 40 university students shows just this occurrence. The sleep-deprived group rated neutral stimuli as negative. *(That sounds exactly like me without sleep!)* [16]

There's something I really don't want to admit here, but I feel like I should. I have needlessly raised my voice at my little guy, and I'm convinced that 95% of those errors were fueled by sleep deprivation. If I couldn't summon up enough reasons to get sleep for myself, Holden was reason enough. He deserved better from me.

Willpower

The other major change I noticed in my chronic, sleep-deprived state was my lack of willpower. As a night-shift nurse, I routinely ate Skittles and Reese Cups for breakfast. Throughout the next day, I'd feast on muffins, toast, McGriddles, and cookies. *(Hangs head in shame.)*

Not surprisingly, my poor choices are backed by research. One study of 30 men and women showed that comparing day 5 of sleep deprivation to day 5 of adequate sleep meant an average increase by 300 calories per day, and most of those were due to an increase in saturated fat. [17] Multiply that by years of sleep deprivation, and I'd be in trouble!

Even simple tasks like getting up to flip the laundry felt so incredibly difficult to accomplish. I was drained. I was functioning at less than 50% of my rested capacity. The work I had accomplished the night before seemed silly and small compared to the non-productive haze that followed the **48 hours after** an all-nighter.

The Change

Last year, I finally resolved to make sleep a priority in my life.

Everything came into focus after that. Sarah started receiving far less frantic phone calls about our next business move. Instead, I'd actually make a list of large goals, break them down into smaller tasks, and prioritize my tasks each day.

As I worked, I found that I could write for an hour straight without straying. I could schedule posts on social media then slip away, unaffected by the blizzard of other thoughts and ideas out there. My anxiety about growing the business melted away too. In a rested state, I could easily see both the positives and negatives of our current situation.

No longer did I feel panicked that we didn't have a LinkedIn Strategy. No longer did I feel inadequate because our Etsy shop only had one-hundred listings instead of five-hundred. Given our top priority to spend time with our families, we're doing fine. With sleep, I could see the big picture with clarity and continue to strategize the **best** steps to take moving forward.

And my mood? Holden will be the first to tell you how much happier Mommy is these days. I can't remember the last time I raised my voice. When he requires a time-out or some other form of discipline, I can do it calmly. Nothing is really a crisis anymore. This is as it should be. I'm blessed to have a fairly crisis-free life at the moment.

I'm eating healthier now too. Cutting up a cucumber or washing carrots doesn't seem like the insurmountable feat that it once was. I no longer require 5 cups of coffee plus 2 Red Bulls per day. Making good choices, whether it's what I eat or how I spend my time is so much easier when my energy tank is full and my mind is clear.

Sarah recently learned an important concept from the book *Essentialism* by Greg McKeown. As an entrepreneur, it's important to "protect the asset". [18] You are an important asset to both your business and your family! Imagine a spy movie where operatives are working to protect the asset they are assigned to guard. You must protect yourself in the same way. Cue the Mission Impossible music, and if you'd like to throw on a spandex suit, I won't judge! I'm sure you look terrific in it!

When we don't get enough sleep, eat healthy, or take care of ourselves in other important ways each day, it's the same as dragging the Hope Diamond down a gravel road on a chain tied to a pick-up truck! I'm cringing just thinking about it... but sometimes we treat ourselves just this way. If no one's told you lately, you're a diamond in the rough. It's time to dust yourself off and treat that precious commodity of **you** with tender love and care. Let's start by getting more sleep!

Practical Ways to Get More Sleep

- Set a firm deadline for ending your work day. Work like crazy and be done no matter what by your pre-determined end time.
- Set a firm turn-off time for the computer and TV. For me, this is at least 30 minutes before the time I want to be snoozing. Experts suggest 1 hour prior.
- Read right before bed instead of watching TV or using electronics. *(I will say that I often read on my iPad. Still, I notice that*

my brain can calm down and fall asleep much easier compared to watching TV.)

- Change into your comfy bedtime clothes or pajamas two hours before bed to get your brain and body primed.
- Try a cup of decaf tea or another soothing, decaffeinated hot beverage.
- Turn out all the lights. *(If you like to read right up until sleep, use a small book light instead of a brighter lamp.)*
- Write down your top 3 to-do items before bed. Better yet, brain dump all of your thoughts before bed!
- If you're awake one hour later than you planned to be and you're able - set your alarm for a little later. *(Life happens. Better to be well-rested when it happens to you!)*
- Set your alarm without the snooze button. This may stress you out, but mentally, it will force you to wake up and hop right out of bed. Also, you won't waste time on an hour of low-quality sleep. If you truly don't want to get up at five AM and don't have to, then knowing you're without a snooze button might force you to re-evaluate what time you realistically need to wake up.

Sleep Tips from the Brilliant Business Moms Community

"As a stressed out college senior planning my graduation, gainful employment, graduate school and a wedding, I spent about six months unable to fall asleep. I'd have a rough night with my mind racing, and the next night I'd be so scared that I wouldn't sleep that I would make that fear come true. It got so bad that I went to see the school psychiatrist. She suggested that I write down all of my worries in a journal for fifteen minutes in the morning and fifteen minutes in the evening, separated from my scheduled bedtime by a few hours to distance my worry from my sleep. My fifteen minute journal times were used to write down everything I was worried about in the form of prayer, physically practicing 2 Corinthians 10:5 "take every thought captive to obey Christ" (ESV). Throughout the day, when I found myself worrying about something, I told myself "it's not time to worry about that yet", and I was able to schedule that worry to reduce my overall stress. This increased the quality of sleep that I got, and helped me be more intentional with my time and aware of my anxiety."
-Carla Patton of TheResumeEmporium.Etsy.com

"Getting a full nights' sleep does not always happen of course, but when I am tempted to stay up into the wee hours to work, I remind myself that if I do I will most likely not be as productive the next day because of the lack of sleep. So I sort of weigh it out to myself..had I rather work one or two more hours tonight and get more done but be too exhausted to do anything tomorrow night? Or go to bed at a normal hour and be able to get another three-four hours' worth of work done the next day? Before I close up my laptop, I usually type a to-do list for the next night. This usually helps me to not only go to bed, but also get to sleep without tons of ideas and "to-dos" keeping me   up."
-Caitlin   Orman   of CustomDecalsBoutique.Etsy.com

"Before I had a baby, my trick was to put on PJ's, brush teeth, take contacts out, etc. right after dinner. That way I wouldn't procrastinate going to bed as much because all it required was getting my body into bed!"
-Rachel Coley of CanDoKiddo.com

"I have small children, so sometimes getting a good night's sleep just isn't going to happen. If I have a night with little or interrupted sleep, I let myself take a nap with my kids the next day. No

guilt! It makes me a much nicer person, and I get way more done."
-Katie Marie of OrganizingMoms.com

"I've worked many years as night shift RN, so that is hard to undo. If I'm going to be totally honest, I'll tell you that I set an alarm in my phone to go get a glass of wine at 9:30 pm. Then I usually sew or work on the computer for another 30-45 minutes and the wine kicks in and I go to bed. Lame, but it works. My body is naturally programmed to go to bed at 1 am because that's what I did for so many years. My shift was 4-11 pm, so this is how I'm still undoing that programming. I also shower at night and that helps to relax before bed too."
-Amy Gabriel of GabrielsGoodTidings.Etsy.com

Take-Aways

- Sleep-deprivation can cause a lack of focus, increased anxiety, poor mood, and decreased willpower, among a host of other health problems!
- By getting enough sleep each night, you will be more productive in the long-run by setting your mind, mood, and ability to focus up for success.
- Grab some of our strategies for getting more sleep and start protecting the precious asset that is **you**!
- If you have a newborn, we're here for you! Enjoy that precious little baby and worry about sleep at a later time.

Chapter 11: The Beauty of Naptime
-Sarah

If you have young children, having a naptime for your child and the ability to simply lay kids down to sleep is the single best way to gain productive work time for your business or big goal. If you are beyond the nap time years or like cranky babies, feel free to skip this chapter!

The inspiration for this chapter is drawn largely on my own experiences. However, I also relied on the book, *Sleep: What Every Parent Needs to Know* by Rachel Y. Moon, MD, FAAP and the American Academy of Pediatrics (AAP). [19] This book by the AAP is evidence based and it draws its conclusions from research studies. Since I am just a mom who has been through the trenches, not an expert, please read more about these topics or discuss them with your pediatrician. I highly recommend this book to aid you in helping your child sleep. It is a straightforward guide filled with practical strategies that work.

Why Naptime Matters

Lest you think this chapter is motivated purely by selfishness for productive work time, the end result of implementing these suggestions is a baby who is happy and sleeping well and a mom who is happy and sleeping well. Healthy sleep habits are good for children and help make happier moms.

I am so blessed to have such a terrific mom in my life. One thing Mom taught me very early on, even before my first child was born, was the importance of good naptime and bedtime sleep habits for kids. Children thrive on routine, and from the day my oldest was born, I knew I wanted to get her on a napping schedule. Newborns don't know they need to be on a napping schedule, nor is it possible for them to be on a schedule early on, so patience is key. But from early on I was determined to get Lilly on a schedule that we could both count on.

Sarah Gilcher of PerennialPlanner.com has worked to get her newest arrival to nap on the same schedule as her older two. She says, "With my third child (3 months) I mostly have her on schedule with the older two children for the afternoon naptime and bedtime. Sometimes that involves waking her up from her morning nap if it is going too late or keeping her up an extra 20 minutes even if she is getting a little crabby." I remember doing similar things as well. Working towards all children napping at the same time is key for mom's sanity and productivity.

I could speak eloquently for hours about the benefits of naptime -- ask any of my friends! Well-rested kids tend to be happier kids, and happy kids are more fun than crabby kids. A nap allows the kids to get through the day without an evening meltdown, which I like to avoid at any cost. The benefit for moms is the peace, quiet, and uninterrupted time. Having a few moments of peace gave me the energy I needed to manage the rest of the day, hopefully with a smile and not a scowl.

Naptime is my power hour of quiet for working on my business goals. I avoid the email and social media rabbit hole and head straight to my big project of the day. I feel an urgency not to waste this precious time. Phone calls? No way. Checking off small items from my list? Not a chance! Housework during naptime? Not around here. I can sweep floors and wash dishes while talking with my kids and attending to their needs. I can fold laundry and vacuum a floor when the kids are up and awake. When I have a chunk of time, especially interruption-free quiet, I head straight for the big business stuff that requires my full concentration. When naptime is done, I know I've worked on my big task and can switch my focus back to kids and the house.

Some of you are reading this and saying, "That may be great for you, but my kids won't nap." I am not a sleep expert or a doctor, so feel free to disregard what I am about to say, but I think most kids can nap. It just may take some work.

In the book *Sleep*, Dr. Rachel Y. Moon states that, "I am convinced that every child wants to sleep well. And sleeping well is something that you often have to teach your child. It is not something that just happens." [19]

As parenthood approached, I didn't realize that getting kids to nap, nap on a schedule, or fall asleep on their own would actually take work. I thought it would happen naturally. I didn't realize that I would have to put in some time teaching my kids how to sleep, but those few hours of teaching has paid dividends in hundreds of hours of quiet. Some of the myths you might currently believe about your baby's sleep habits may be proven false if you can spend some time teaching your baby to sleep. Imagine the time you will gain when you can just lay your baby in the crib to sleep instead of rocking or nursing for 30 minutes beforehand. Think about the time you will gain when your baby naps for 2 hours instead of 30 minutes. Think of what your baby will gain in added rest. I was there, and I have seen the other side, and it is bliss!

One of the most important things to teach your baby is how to fall asleep on their own. The experts call this "self-soothing". After your baby has passed the early infancy stage, begin to teach your baby to fall asleep on their own.

When your baby is little, they often fall asleep nursing or drinking their bottle, and then you lay them down in their crib already asleep. This may work like a dream when they are little, but as your baby gets older this will happen less and less often, and you are left rocking the baby for seemingly endless minutes until they do fall asleep. To avoid this, *Sleep* says, "We...recommend that babies be placed in their cribs while drowsy but still awake . . . This helps link being in the crib with the pleasant feeling of falling asleep. (Psychologists call this forming a positive sleep association.)" [19]

When your baby is looking drowsy while taking a bottle or nursing, but has not yet fallen asleep, lay the baby down in the crib and tiptoe out of the room. The first few times, the baby will probably come out of their doze and begin to cry. Wait a few minutes, go back in, and comfort your baby, but try to avoid picking up your baby from the crib. This may need to happen several times before the baby falls asleep for the night.

The next night do the same thing. *Sleep* says "When your baby is calm again but still awake, put her back in her crib, say your good-nights, and leave her side. If she cries again after you leave, give her a few minutes to settle on her own. Many babies go to sleep more quickly if left for a while. If the crying keeps up, repeat your visits at increasingly longer intervals, but no longer than 10 minutes at a time. . . If you pick her up, your baby will expect a lengthy cuddle and will redouble her crying when you place her down again; sleepiness will be delayed even further."

Crying it out often comes with a bad reputation, but in my experience, after only a few nights of laying the baby down awake, and only letting the baby cry for a few minutes at a time, my baby could fall asleep on her own. Marathon sessions of crying or weeks of agony to train her to fall asleep never materialized. Many people attach a bad feeling to crying it out without ever actually trying it. I found it to be far less work than I imagined, with far less tears. *Sleep* says "It generally takes 3 to 5 nights for your baby to fall asleep without too much fuss." [19] I hope the same holds true for you.

Teaching a baby to fall asleep on their own creates several benefits. The first is that you gain the time you would normally spend trying to get the baby to fall asleep. Boy have I been there! One creak from the floor as you tip toe out of the room and you're sunk!

Second, the experts say that teaching a baby to fall asleep on their own helps the baby to stay asleep during the night. When a baby falls asleep in mother's arms, but wakes up in their crib, they are startled, and don't remember how they got from one place to another. When a baby falls asleep on their own and then wakes up, they are not startled, and already have the skills to fall back asleep. Yeah! High-fives! *(Oh wait, the baby is sleeping...air high-fives!)* More sleep for baby means more sleep for you! More sleep for you results in more productivity for your home, business, big goal, or passion. See, you forgot why we were talking about napping in the first place, but it all comes around!

Third, although it sounds so relaxing to rock your baby to sleep every single night, it can be stressful. Wondering if they are deeply asleep enough to lay them down, being bone tired but continuing to rock on, having your husband checking to see if baby's eyes are closed, these routines become stressful if needed at every naptime and bedtime.

Another sleep problem I encountered was a baby waking up after only a very short afternoon nap. Charity, my second baby, had this issue. I would lay her down for her afternoon nap, she would fall asleep and sleep for 45 minutes, and wake up crying.

Since she was my baby #2, I was expecting long afternoon naps of 2 or 3 hours. A 45 minute nap was killing me! Barely had I started anything before I had a crying baby again. I was tempted to pick her up and call an end to the naptime. I might have if she was my first baby, however I was a little wiser now and knew that longer naps were possible. I would pick her up, settle her down, rock her a little, and lay her back down. Most of the time she would fall back asleep and give me another 45 minutes. Sometimes she didn't and we would try it again, soothing and laying down. This short 45 minute nap routine seemed to continue forever. Eventually, that baby girl learned to just stay asleep. Hallelujah! My nice long 2 or 3 hour nap times were back! It took time and effort, but the hours I gained far surpassed the hours I spent training her to sleep!

You may be thinking that teaching your baby how to sleep and nap sounds like too much work. After all, it only takes you 30 minutes a night to get your baby to sleep, that's really not that much time. But 30 minutes x 365 days is 182 hours! Talk about finding a magic pill to create more time! *(Anyone know how to bottle up baby sleep and sell it......? That would make a killer Etsy listing!)*

Still not convinced? Are you waiting for your kids to grow out of needing help to sleep? I have known many parents who each night must lay down with their older preschool child until they fall asleep. The book *Sleep* even mentioned a case of a teenager sleeping in their parent's bed! [19] I enjoy tucking my kids into bed, kissing them goodnight, turning out the light, and closing the door. Simplicity is divine!

Naptime has evolved as we had more children, and as they grew older. When my oldest began to outgrow her naps in the preschool years, I still insisted on a quiet time. During quiet time she played with toys quietly in her room, while her younger sister and brother napped. Now I have only one child who naps sporadically, but I still keep the quiet time schedule. Because naptime and quiet time have been a part of our everyday lives for nearly 8 years, the kids accept it. They know quiet time is a normal part of every day. My older two escape quiet time when they are at school during the week, but when the weekend arrives, quiet time is back! The same hold true for summer vacation. I don't think I could survive summer vacation without quiet time!

I am not alone in the use of quiet time for older preschoolers or elementary age children. Anne Bogel of ModernMrsDarcy.com still has a quiet time in her household for reading. Her kids are all elementary age, and homeschooled, but every day they have a quiet reading time.

Regardless of the age, everyone benefits from some quiet. Carve out a time of peace in your day.

If you're a mom trying to build a business or fulfill a dream, having a quiet time and kids that will sleep will aid you tremendously in accomplishing those dreams. This chapter was written during quiet time! I can keep writing now that everyone is back downstairs and playing, but my rate of writing will certainly slow down. The time saved by teaching kids to fall asleep, and sticking with a naptime could be key in allowing you to pursue your big dreams and passions. We are mixing motherhood with business around here, for spectacular results!

Here's what our Brilliant Business Moms Community had to say about naptime:

Julia Fain of TagandTibby.com says, "We don't have nappers anymore, but our kids go to bed early (usually at 7:30 pm). We read stories, have a short prayer time, and then I still have time to work a little at night and spend time with my husband. It works so well for us!"

Katie Marie of OrganizingMoms.com says, "We have twins, so we've always been really consistent about routines for bedtime. We try to do almost the same thing every day, and the kids know what to expect. They're so good at their bedtime routines that they can tell their babysitters what steps are next when they're putting them to bed. To keep them in bed, we ended up using a clock that turns green when it's time to wake up. Don't tell, but we set it for 30 minutes later during Christmas break, and it still works like a charm!"

Brittany Adkison of BrittanysBest.com says, "The key to getting our son to sleep is a consistent schedule. When our son went through a short or no-napping phase at about 4 months, we read a ton of books on sleep. We took the advice to put him to sleep in his crib only. That meant no napping in the car, swing, or carrier. We have a naptime and bedtime routine that we follow all the time. We very rarely deviate from the schedule – I mean VERY RARELY! He has an early bedtime, 7:30 pm. When he started to resist naps as a toddler, we let him know that he doesn't have to sleep but he does need to be in his crib/bed for a "rest" every day – he ends up sleeping about 95% of his "rests".

Take-Aways

- Teaching your kids to sleep does take work, but the end results are worth it!
- When children outgrow naptime, have a quiet time instead.
- By teaching children to sleep and nap well, you will gain hundreds of hours of quiet to pursue your passions and goals.
- Well rested children are happy children!

Chapter 12: Spending Your Days with Little Ones (How to Thrive!)
-Sarah

As a mom entrepreneur working from home with kids buzzing around, finding new ways to carve out focused time is essential. My days run more smoothly when I am focused on one thing at a time. More cleaning gets done if I avoid distractions. If I tackle that business To Do list with a singular purpose, I get more done in less time. Quality time with my kids is enjoyed more fully when I give them my full attention.

The key is gaining that distraction-free time, which can feel next to impossible with many little voices clamoring for attention.

Here are a few tips to help you gain some distraction free time with little ones around:

Victoria Wilson of VictoriaEasterWilson.com sagely notes "Make sure you're fully present in your kid's day (ex. not checking Facebook incessantly while playing with them). This helps kids not feel neglected when you really do have to focus on something else. I've noticed that my daughter allows me to work when I HAVE to do something if I've previously given her full attention."

Related to that idea, Ellen Russell of CreateInTheChaos.com says, "We've taught them that there are times when they need to go play and entertain themselves. It's such a good skill for them to have in general."

Consider swapping kid watching with a friend who lives nearby. Is it that more difficult or more time consuming to watch 4 kids compared to your 2? Not generally. How much progress toward a business goal can you make with 2 hours of uninterrupted quiet time? Quite a bit! Gaining a few hours every week can help you reach your business goals.

Does a local church have a mother's day out program? Many churches allow you to drop off your kids for a few hours for a nominal fee. This tactic might be especially helpful in the summer when school and preschool are no longer in session.

It's amazing the amount of toys our children have and yet they still regularly declare that they are bored! Hide several toys and pull them out when its crunch time with your business. They are toys the kids haven't seen for a while so they will seem fresh and new. It might help to occupy them while you complete an important project.

Lee Ann Taylor of LeeAnnGTaylor.com uses this technique. "We bought an inexpensive easel that has paper on one side and a chalk board on the other. We tuck it away so that when we bring it out for my kids to play with (5 and 2) it's like having something new to play with."

When the kids are on break from school, Kelly Meyer of HoleySocksArt.com says, "I give the kids the choice of "fun first" or "fun later". I've made it clear that just because they are on break doesn't mean I get to be. I still have some work to do, but I have the luxury to be flexible about it."

Along those same lines, "We start the day by

making a plan where each child gets to decide a few things they want to do with mommy. I spread these little "play-breaks" throughout the day and since they know that mommy will stop and give them attention when it is time, they contentedly play with one another in between. It doesn't always work perfectly, so I try to take cues from my kids. On days they seem to need more I give them more, they are my first priority after all." That is fantastic advice from Sarah Koontz of GroundedandSurrounded.com.

One of the easiest ways to distract my kids in the summer is to freeze some of their toys in Tupperware containers filled water. I pull out the tubs of frozen toys, hand them some plastic tools, and let them go to work trying to dig out the toys. This all happens on the porch where I can still keep an eye on them. They love this, but it's so simple and costs me nothing!

Veronica Armstrong of GabriellasDesigns.com says, "When I need to be in my office sewing or designing during the day, I like to roll out butcher paper on the floor and give my toddler crayons or colored pencils. She loves laying out on her belly and drawing. I also keep lots of dollar store stickers on hand because just putting stickers on the paper can entertain her for a while too. I like it too because then I can take mini breaks to color with her."

What works for one child will not always work for another says Katie Clark of KatieDidProductions.com so keep trying various ideas, "My kids are so different! My daughter was content for at least an hour with coloring, stickers, paints or anything else artistic. My son? Not so much. He is only interested in snacks or sometimes a pile of pots, pans, measuring cups, bowls and spoons." I love the snacks idea, so true!

If you have a toddler that is in the get-into-everything stage, you might want try this tip from Lauree Sayne of DancingDishAndDecor.com, "When she was little and first started using coloring books and crayons the rule was she could only color in her high chair. That kept her both happy and confined." Lauree's daughter who is now in her teens has blossomed into a very talented artist.

For very young kids you may want to try Katy Erickson's idea, "My 7 month old's current favorite is "the pot of gold": a pot full of canning lid rings. She enjoys the sounds the lids make against the pot, the wood floor, and each other. I switch it up and periodically fill the pot with all kinds of "treasures" from the kitchen, like lids, spoons, water bottles, and small cloth sacks." Katy blogs from her converted school bus at CatchingEddies.com.

Rachel Coley of CanDoKiddo.com *(who by the way is a pediatric Occupational Therapist)* has some really fun ideas for her 9 month old son, "I make mischief corners around the house...a box of socks, an empty coffee can with wood blocks in it, an empty cardboard egg carton with golf balls in it, a bath loofah hanging from a doorknob. He has little interest in real toys these days and much prefers stumbling upon something new and mysterious."

Jamie Swenka of The30Things.com says, "I let my kids 'help' if possible. I'll give them specific roles that they can do that are for the business. Even if it might take me a few minutes to complete, it can take them 30. I'll even 'pay' them for their time. I have 2 girls age 3 & 4 and a 1 year old boy. I hope I am teaching my girls (and boy when he's older) that they can do business!"

Sarah Gilcher of PerennialPlanner.Etsy.com has lots of unique ideas. "Any directed but creative play helps like the moldable sand with ice cream tools, or "Counting Bears" - they come with colored sorting cups and multicolored bears. They play with them for a long time. Stickers, markers, paper, ask them to make menus for a restaurant then order food from them and have them prepare it in their play kitchen. Sometimes I ask my girls to fix my hair while I sit at my computer, they love to spray it with water and brush and clip!"

"I have four kids and now my youngest is at home by himself while the others are at school. He kind of doesn't like not getting all my attention, so I've tried two different options besides screen time that seem to work. First, I talk to him about what I need to do and get done. I tell him that he can be in the same room as me, but I need him to be quiet and play by himself. Then, I limit myself to the one task that needs to get done, take a break to play, and then do another task. The other thing that I do is I have some favorite, special toys for those times when I am interviewing a person for an article. He doesn't get those things at all unless we are out and about and I'm having an important discussion. In fact the other kids don't even know about them." Great tips from Gianna Kordatsky of FamilyFunTwinCities.com

When the weather is nice, don't forget some outdoor activities.   Ashley   Monda   of

OurFullTable.com says, "My son loves his outdoor water table. Give him a bunch of cups to pour water around and it's a good hour plus of quality work time!"

Katy Campbell of LittleRedFlag.Etsy.com has both indoor and outdoor ideas she employs. "We invested in outdoor toys for our fenced backyard so I could send the boys out to play in the sandbox or on the swing set which I can view from the kitchen table while I work on my laptop, sketch or plan. One of the best indoor activities, hands down, is building a tent. My boys will grab pillows, stuffed animals, flashlights, books, cars, sippy cups, you name it, and crawl under there and have great adventures and I undoubtedly will hear lots of giggles."

When you absolutely need some quiet for your project, Meredith Marsh of GoProMom.com has been known to do work in a unique location. "I have taken my laptop into the bathroom to record a screencast. I put it on the back of the toilet, and sit backwards on it with the lid down. Really awkward! But, worth it to get it done when you need to just get it done."

When Stephanie O'Dea of StephanieODea.com received an important business phone call, she placed her toddler in a dry bath tub and handed her a tub of frosting and spoon! The toddler was safe and entertained so that Stephanie could complete the 10 minute phone call.

Another time saver I've employed recently is refusing to referee my children's arguments. I got so tired of having to jump in, wade through the facts, and pronounce a verdict. It took time and it drained me. Now when they start calling "Mom, so-and-so did something to me!" My reply is almost always, "Work it out!" If they can't work it out and continue fighting, they go to their rooms to cool off.

This parenting technique has helped me so much, and I think it's good for the kids. They learn to get along and resolve conflicts on their own. If someone isn't playing nice, the other kids can simply choose not to play with that child for a while. This method saves me the emotional trauma of figuring out what's going on and what should be done about it. I am not saying that I don't discipline when appropriate. Believe me, plenty of that still happens. But so many kids' squabbles are frivolous. Refusing to referee has saved me time and frustration.

To sneak in a little "me" time when your kids are older, consider Rhonda's advice from

MultiTaskingMaven.com "We live in a small town so I commute to all sporting activities and use this time for "My Education". I have a podcast or YouTube video I listen/watch every day. While the kids are practicing soccer, baseball or computer class, I am writing blog posts and planning."

This isn't kid related but another way to gain time could be to trade skills. Are you a graphic designer and your friend is a whiz at bookkeeping? Consider trading skills and services to help each other grow your businesses. When you trudge through a task that is not your strong suit, it takes longer, and feels burdensome. By skill swapping you will get better results than you imagined, in less time, at no cost. A triple win!

The goal of all of this is not to find clever ways to not spend any time with your kids! The goal is to make good use of our time, so that every day there's an opportunity to put our computers away and spend focused, quality time with our kids. I don't want to be a mom who always has her head buried in her computer or on the phone. I want to work hard when I'm working, play hard when I'm playing, and be fully focused on each. I think you can see from these tips that the kids of other mom entrepreneurs are sure having a lot of fun!

Take-Aways

- As a mamapreneur juggling a business and kids, you need to get creative in carving out quality time for both.
- By having more focus on each task, a better result is achieved.
- Get creative and find ways to keep the kids entertained! You'll achieve more in your business and have more down time to spend with your family!

Chapter 13: Multi-Task Less, Achieve More
-Beth Anne

Multi-tasking.   As moms, we wear it like a badge of honor.   We listen to podcasts while rinsing dishes, teaching our child multiplication tables, talking to our sister on the phone, and stirring a pot on the stove. We snicker while we watch our husbands try to hold a conversation while feeding the baby and entertaining the preschooler. "Uhhhh, ummm.... I can't remember what I was saying....."   "What an amateur!" we think.

Multi-tasking.   Most of us think we're just so **good** at it!   We pride ourselves on it – thinking that the better we get at multi-tasking, the more productive we can be. Multitasking seems to be a rite of passage for most moms. If you weren't great at it before you had children, you'll quickly don the uniform, head off to multi-tasking school, and learn how to juggle five tasks like the best of 'em!

I hate to burst your bubble and rip that badge off of your chest, but the scientific studies on the topic are about to prove you wrong. Multi-tasking does not help you to be more productive, it's a hindrance in most situations.

Does this scene look familiar?

You're sewing a new product for your shop or writing a new blog post, and "ding!" that phone of yours has exciting, important news to share! Could it be a new heart on Instagram?! Did someone comment on your Facebook post?! Maybe, *(joy of all joys!)*, you got a new follower on Pinterest!!! You drop everything, run to your phone, pushing toddlers and toys out of your way, to check on this ground breaking update. Turns out, it's a new email! A new email?!?! Whaaaaaaaaaaat?!?! "This is the most exciting day of my life!" you think, "It's like Drew Carey just told me to "c'mon down to the Price is Right!!!"

If this sounds ridiculous, you're right. It is. But how many of us truly act like it's the most urgent, exciting, and necessary thing in the whole world when our phone pings with a new notification? I'm right there with you, friends. I'm so guilty, but armed with the facts, I'm committed to doing better.

A 2013 Internet Trends Report indicates that mobile users reach for their phones one-hundred and fifty times per day. Yes, you read that correctly, one-five-zero! Even when you control for eighteen instances of checking the time, and a few instances of using your camera or perhaps even a productivity app, the blended average of social sessions per day per smart phone user was fifty-one times. [20]

Unless you run a telemarketing firm and your business relies on phone calls for revenue, this number should not be ok with you. Even on my most idea-ridden days I might call Sarah four times, my husband two times, and my mom once. Let's add in two calls to doctors for Holden, a call from another friend, and I'm still left with forty-one instances of either checking social media, my email, or texting. Yikes!

I'm fairly confident that on a few occasions I have been there, but I don't want to be there again. Nothing on my phone is really important enough to take up that much of my day. I have the sweetest little boy sitting right in front of me, and he matters so much more. If I'm not working on my business, I should be spending time with him. That cute photo of my friend's child on Facebook can absolutely wait because I'm too busy making memories with my own adorable guy.

Another scenario that's even more tempting for me: I'm writing a chapter for our book. I have one hour of complete quiet and solitude to myself. This is a rare and precious commodity. I've committed to write like the wind. I sit down, and the words flow like sweet tea on a hot southern day. Two pages are done before I even realize it. One thousand words - **bam**! I'm fist-pumping the air and feeling great. Then... I hit a roadblock. I can't quite figure out what I want to say next or how to say it in just the right way.

I feel my brain straining under the task. It's similar to the tension I feel when I try to lift forty pounds over my head at the gym. *(Did I mention that I'm a wimp?)* Aaaaahhhh... it's painful.... I don't want to do it.... I'm shaking under the strain....I'd rather give up! Oh boy, I've got the best idea! I'll just switch over to email real quick and give my brain a break, because that's important too. No big deal. Let me check my email and then I'll get right back to work!

Usually one of two things happens: thirty minutes later my writing time is up and I haven't written another word since I first switched over to email. Or I check and answer one email, get back to work, only to find myself switching back to email, Facebook, and Twitter several more times during the course of that hour.

Every time I switch back and forth, I'm forcing my brain to do more work. I'm requiring it to shift attention and direction from one task to another. This is called the "switching cost". [21] What happens feels quite similar to that moment when you walk into a room and ask, "What did I come in here to get? Why am I standing here?" I can't remember. I can't focus and stay on-track. I'm giving so much less than my best effort to my work, and I'm taking so much more time to get it done.

I don't expect you to take my word for it, so instead I have a few studies to share. I love the one I'm sharing next. Thirteen information workers were cut off from using their email for five days. Their work habits were measured before and during the study. The participants even wore heart-rate monitors to measure their stress levels. They completed self-reported surveys as well.

The results really aren't that surprising, but perhaps hearing them will make all of us reconsider our own work habits. Without email, the workers switched between computer windows much less and stayed focused on the same task much longer. Without that handy little distraction tool at their disposal, when they felt like copping out, they simply didn't. They kept working. Their heart-rate variability was also lower without email, indicating that they were less stressed. [22]

Here's another scenario I attempt to get away with too often. I try to learn something new while the TV or music is blaring in the background. Maybe it's a special day and Holden gets to watch a movie, or Chris has worked a really long day, and he's ready to relax with a show. I'm in the same room, trying to read a book about business, or read someone's really helpful blog post about Etsy selling.

One study showed that when the TV was playing the background, it was more difficult for participants to later recall what they had learned.

[23] They could recognize it, sure, but as a business owner, you need to make sure that the time you spend learning something new will stay in your memory forever. Recognizing it when you see that strategy again on another blog won't do you much good. You need to be able to internalize that information and act on it when the time is right.

I know that you're doing the best you can. You're a mom and quiet is as rare as a sparkling floor in your house. I'm sharing this example to suggest that there are other, more rote tasks that you could do during these times, such as interact on social media or edit your photos. However, if you're truly trying to learn and retain something new, the TV, music, or noisy kids will make the process much less effective.

There are those of us who believe that we've been multi-tasking for so long, that we're truly good at it. We're old pros! We've re-wired our brains, and multi-tasking is second nature. "Beth Anne" you're saying, "I get that you're a new mom. You're still a rookie in this world, an infant, really, but when you've been at this as long as I have, you'll get the hang of it."

Unfortunately, those annoying men and women in the lab coats are shaking their heads yet again. One such white-coat, Clifford Nass, performed a study out of Stanford in 2009. He recruited 262 college students. He gave them all questionnaires to assess the level of media multi-tasking they do on a regular basis. He whittled his test group down to 41 total students. Half of those students were heavy media multi-taskers while half were light media multi-taskers. Media multi-taskers are defined as people who frequently consume two or more forms of media at once. Examples of media would be music, television, social media, phone calls, emails, or print.

The two groups were taken through a series of tests and activities to measure different cognitive skills. Surprisingly enough, the low media multi-taskers, those who seldom, for example, listen to music while writing emails and texting a friend, were actually **better** at focusing in the face of distractions than were the heavy media multi-taskers.

The two groups were taken through a series of tests and activities to measure different cognitive skills. I won't bore you with the details, but the tests involved activities like noticing the position of different-colored rectangles amidst X's, or noticing if a two-letter pair was the "right one" or "wrong one."

According to test results, bombarding one's brain with multiple forms of media often makes it **more** difficult for the brain to discern which stimuli require the most attention and which distracting stimuli to block. [24]

The more time you spend each day allowing multiple forms of media, such as phone calls, music, texting, social media, the TV, talking, or reading, to enter your brain simultaneously, the worse your brain becomes at focusing on a task. There is no way I'll allow my brain to get worse at the ability to focus. We're already struggling with Mommy Brain, right? We can't afford to make frequent multi-tasking part of our lives and further degrade our already overwhelmed brains!

These studies (and many more like them!) are enough to make me take notice. I'm making a deliberate effort to slow down, eliminate distractions, and add quiet to my day.

Is Multi-Tasking Ever Ok?

There are some cases when multi-tasking can be acceptable, but only when one of your tasks is physical, mindless work, while the other task engages your brain. I haven't yet seen a study that shows any harmful effects to this practice, but if I do, you'll be the first to know!

For example, I often play a podcast in the kitchen while I'm rinsing dishes. Holden is in the living room playing, and if he needs something or wants to chat it's easy enough to push pause. On some days this means I push pause 20 times in a 30-minute period! Usually, on those days, I simply decide that my family needs more of my attention than I anticipated, and I save the podcast for another time.

On the flip-side, knowing that I get to listen to podcasts while I do tasks that serve my family makes those tasks feel so much more enjoyable. In general, I love to clean the house while I have my cell phone in my pocket and listen to an audiobook. I need all the motivation I can get to make cleaning a priority, and learning something new or even listening to a novel does the trick. And who knows - Holden may be picking up on a few business tips while he drives his cars all over the living room!

After outlining point after point on the dangers of multi-tasking, I feel like the Surgeon General preaching to you about the dangers of cigarettes! Multi-tasking is bad; don't do it. Now that you're armed with knowledge about how our brains work and how multi-tasking can affect them, I hope you will change some of your habits, be more focused, and have a healthier brain.

Take-Aways

- Multi-tasking is generally less effective in helping you to get things done.
- Refuse to toggle between windows to check email or social media while you're working on important tasks and big goals.
- Engaging in multiple forms of media at once will decrease your ability to learn and your ability to focus over time.
- If some form of media is on, use that time to do work that doesn't require too much brain power.
- Pairing a mental task with a physical task is a better solution for multi-tasking.

Chapter 14: How Your Environment, Rewards, and the Zone Can Help you Get More Done!
-Sarah

I haven't always believed that creating the right work environment played an important role in time management and productivity, but I'm now convinced. For instance, I've been putting off writing my portions of this book. I've been busy, but that never changes. So today, I told myself, "Sarah, during naptime, when you have a quiet house, then you can have your cup of coffee **only** if you are sitting down to write. Plus you can have a few almond Hershey kisses!"

All day I've been visualizing that quiet time of my day and looking forward to sitting down and writing. I pulled a little table over to the rocking chair, prepared my French press, and unwrapped my kisses. I was looking forward to that quiet in my day, looking out the window while I got my thoughts down on "paper" and sipping my specially-bought caramel flavored Starbucks coffee.

Just thinking of that lovely environment and the rewards I had planned, had me looking forward to writing all day. Compare that to an uncomfortable chair, a dark room, and no soothing drink to sip. The right environment can put you in the mood to get serious work done.

I also have a hard time getting down to work if the house is too messy. I am no neat freak, Beth Anne can attest to that! Most of my work occurs at the kitchen table because I don't have an office. If sandwich crumbs and jelly were missed at lunch clean up, it's difficult for me to focus and accomplish anything of significance until I wipe down the table.

Anne Bogel of ModernMrsDarcy.com has a

great tip for making your home look tidier in much less time. She runs around putting everything that's out of place into an empty laundry basket. Then, she stows that basket in a corner of the room until she has enough dedicated time to put everything away. Immediately, that room looks 10x neater, but she didn't have to waste precious work time. That tidy environment? I bet she gets more focused work done than if she left everything scattered around the room. [25]

Dana Regehr of JanieLaneStudio.Etsy.com also needs a tidy environment to be her most productive. "I like my space to be clean and organized. It gets messy as I go, but it needs to be clean when I start."

Sometimes it All Comes Down to Rewards

I used to be the worst ever at getting laundry folded. Starting laundry, not a problem, but folding it...forget it! Then I discovered that Matlock was on at 10am, and I love Matlock! I got in the habit of doing laundry every Friday. I would do 3 loads of laundry that morning, and have 3 loads to fold at the same time, all while I watched Matlock. No Matlock at other times, only when I was folding laundry. I started to look forward to folding laundry. When they cancelled the Matlock reruns, I turned to audio books. Knowing that I can hear more of my book if I'm folding laundry makes me do laundry a lot more often than I used to! The chore has now become a pleasure.

For our Etsy shop, The Amateur Naturalist (TheAmateurNaturalist.Etsy.com), I'm in charge of packaging and shipping. I don't enjoy packaging our terrarium kits. Packaging is a monotonous task and the supplies are in our cold, dark, windowless basement, but audio books and podcasts have turned the chore of packaging into a pleasure.

I look forward to telling my husband, "Honey I need to go package for a couple of hours in the basement. Can you hold down the fort?" My work environment isn't ideal, but I've created a reward by adding audio books and podcasts. I've set the stage to get work done.

I'm not the only one who loves a good audiobook! Helen Xia of HelenXiaHandmade.Etsy.com loves listening to audio books! "I just redeemed a free month at Audible and I love it! I'm actually enjoying it more than Podcasts because drawing & painting can take hours and I don't like having to start a new podcast on a completely different subject every

30 minutes."

Melissa Kaiserman of ATime4Everything.Etsy.com loves to use environmental influences and rewards to motivate her. She says, "As far as environmental factors that help motivate me, I have a radiant heat dish near my sewing table so that I stay comfortable, I make sure lighting is plentiful, and I have arranged my studio so that the location of everything makes the best sense with my workflow and prevents me from having to do unnecessary zigzagging around the room. (This has taken a bit of trial and error, but it's so worth it.) As far as rewards, I'll determine a certain amount of time I have to work or a certain number of items or days' worth of orders I have to finish cutting or sewing before I can go get a cup of coffee, sit down with a book for 15 minutes, etc. Or I'll tell myself that if I can get the orders that have to go out on a certain day finished and packaged by that morning rather than right before the post office closes, then I can spend a couple of hours working on something like online research for an idea--which I love and which can so often distract me! Oh, and I almost forgot: Listening to podcasts and watching movies (preferably a long series) are huge motivators for me as well. When I don't really feel like doing a task, I can quickly change my mindset when I start listening to or watching something enjoyable!"

Coffee and chocolate seem to be recurring theme when it comes to motivation to work! Sarah Gilcher of PerennialPlanner.Etsy.com says that "A bit of chocolate and coffee to sit down to makes work time quite the haven!" Amen sister!

A personal favorite motivator of mine is echoed by Katie Clark of KatieDidProductions.com, "I'm a big fan of to-do lists. There's something so satisfying about crossing a task off the list. The more I do, the more momentum I gain to do more."

Do you need more extrinsic motivations to grow your business or pursue your passions? Try teaming up with a like-minded friend *(or sister!)*. Knowing that Beth Anne is counting on me to get a job done is highly motivating. Plus, when I feel discouraged, she is there to give me a pep talk, and vice-versa. Another huge benefit of teaming up is that more can be accomplished in a shorter time. If you play to each other's strengths, some of the tasks you hate doing, can be accomplished by a partner who is jazzed to complete that task. Gianna Kordatzsky of FamilyFunTwinCities.com agrees, "Being part of a team helps to motivate me." Gianna approached two women she didn't know about combining forces, and the results have been amazing!

Most days, setting up my environment and creating rewards can really get me going on the task at hand. Other days, something else entirely kicks in!

The Zone

Every once in a while I seem to enter "The Zone", a super human state of being where tasks get accomplished at an outstanding rate of speed! Ever happen to you?

Something just comes over me and powerful forces drive me to tackle projects I often avoid. I do my best to go with the flow when I'm in the zone, as long as my schedule can allow me the flexibility.

For instance, the other day, I noticed a drip down my kitchen cabinet, and I began to wipe it down. I felt the urge to keep going and wipe down more cabinets. Normally I don't have the urge to wipe down kitchen cabinets, so I went with it and every cabinet in the kitchen was cleaned. What a good feeling! It hardly felt like work at all.

The same thing applies when I am in a

purging or organizing mood. Sometimes I go to clean out a closet and find that I don't want to throw anything away. Another day I may look at the same closet and be willing to get rid of many things.   Whether it is cleaning, purging, organizing, writing, or bookkeeping; being in the mood makes a huge difference. When the mood strikes, ride it out!

One caveat, make sure being in the zone isn't taking you away from a big task you need to accomplish, or a nagging item you have been putting off. If you're in the zone to online shop instead of knitting that new hat for your Etsy shop, abandon the zone!

If you're dealing with a creative block, getting up and doing something productive, like cleaning out a messy drawer might be the quick win you need to get yourself going again. Rather than sit and stare at a screen for 20 minutes while your eyes go numb, get moving, secure a quick win, and get your creative juices flowing.

Finding ways to make your environment and work more enjoyable can help you to be more productive.   Instead of putting off boring, unfulfilling chores, you'll be motivated to tackle them, and maybe even look forward to them! Use your environment, rewards, and the zone to your advantage. They are all useful tools to encourage focus and productivity. Let me know if you find any tricks to make cleaning toilets enjoyable, I still need help with that one!!

Take-Aways

- A tidy and enjoyable work environment can help your mind stay focused.
- Give yourself special rewards during work time to make work more fun!
- When you're in the zone, ride it out! You'll be much more productive.

Chapter 15: The Power of the Clock & Other Tricks for Getting More Done
-Beth Anne

In chapter fourteen, Sarah discussed how a clean, happy, and rewarding environment can improve your productivity. Keeping my house clean is a constant struggle. As a busy mom, I often find that I put off housework and other small tasks in favor of working on our business. I'll think to myself, "Dishes?! I don't have time for that. I have 2 blog posts to write."

By the end of the day, I'm so tired I can hardly keep my eyes open, and the dishes aren't looking any more appealing now that the cheese and ketchup has congealed into a beautiful, gummy paste.

The way I combat this habit of delaying those less appealing tasks is with my ten-minute rule. I give myself a pep talk: "Just ten minutes. All you have to do is spend ten minutes working in the kitchen to make it look better. At the end of ten minutes, you can go back to writing."

My ten-minute rule helps me to accomplish three things:

1. I work much faster knowing that I've only allotted ten minutes for the task.
2. I avoid procrastination by making chores seem so much more do-able. I can do anything for 10 minutes, right?
3. I usually get into the task at hand and spend a few more minutes getting the whole job done!

I have several friends who are great at keeping their homes clean. They can't focus on writing, or editing photos, or any type of computer work until their house and workplace are both pristine. Good for them! I am not one of those people. I wish people like this would live under my stairs and make my house their mission too! Those people would be generously rewarded with giggles, chocolate-faced kisses, and extra sandy messes just as soon as they think their job is done. I know... I know. It's pretty much a dream job. Applications are pouring in.

If you fall into the procrasti-cleaner group, then maybe it's more difficult for you to actually sit down and tackle some of your larger goals like writing a book, starting a blog, or optimizing those Etsy listings for SEO.

If you fall into the latter category, and I'd be insanely jealous of your sparkling windows, then I suggest you use the ten-minute rule in reverse. As you look around your house and see laundry to be folded, counters to be wiped, and floors to be swept, tell yourself, "Just ten minutes. I need to spend just ten minutes tackling my big goal with intensity, and then I can go back to cleaning." You'll probably get into the project and work much more than ten minutes, but if you don't, you will still feel great about tackling that big goal, one step at a time.

I also use the ten-minute rule if I've had an exceptionally crazy day, but I know I need to make progress on my big goal. Just ten minutes before bed works like a dream and improves my sleep too! I no longer feel stressed and disappointed in myself for not making progress on my biggest passion. Winding down from work early in the day is often a great idea, **but**, if you've had one of those days *(you know what I mean!)* pushing yourself to do ten minutes will make you feel better about your day and ease your mind.

When it comes to procrastination and the distracted minds we moms live with every day, there's another rule I love. This one comes from Getting Things Done by David Allen. [3] It's called the two-minute rule. The point of this one is that it wastes a lot of brain power trying to hold all those little tasks and should-do's in your brain for a later time. You're distracted and doing less than your best work when you continue to put off those tiny tasks for later.

Here's where the two-minute rule comes into play: If the task you need to do takes less than two minutes, do it now. As soon as you think of it, put that load of laundry in the dryer. Clear off the breakfast table. Write that quick email. Telling yourself you'll do it later will just take up valuable brain space. Don't even think about it. Don't mull it over. Do it immediately. Get your body in motion and that, in and of itself, will become a habit.

My only exception to this rule is when I've got dedicated quiet time to work on my greatest passion. If it's naptime and I planned to write for two hours, then you'd better believe I'm going to write... not tidytoys/loadthedryer/writemygrocerylist/wipedownthe sink. No way.

If you think of little tasks during your precious, rare, beautiful quiet time, then simply write those tasks down on your running to-do list and get back to work. By writing the task down, you're freeing your mind from having to remember it. You can keep writing, taking photos, sculpting, or whatever that greatest passion is that you're pursuing.

Finally, I have one other trick that works quite well if you're a recovering perfectionist like me. Save your small, but deadline-oriented tasks until just before they are due. I can hear your protests: "What?! Didn't you **just** tell me to avoid procrastination? Isn't this whole chapter about getting work done now?" Yes, dear reader, it is, but hear me out. I'll only take a minute to explain.

I call this trick, Procrasti-planning. If you're someone who punches out tasks like writing blog posts, creating Etsy listings, or editing photos very quickly and easily, you may not need this trick. If that happens to be you, there's a place under my stairs for you too!

Here's how Procrasti-planning works: for the tasks that should be relatively quick and easy, such as creating a great cover photo, or writing an email to send to your list - those tasks turn into hours-long endeavors for perfectionists! Yes. That would be me. I know there are other women out there just like me! We write descriptive, creative prose. Our cover photos are incredible, but we took five times as long as that blogger down the street. Her cover photos still look pretty good, and they still go viral on Pinterest.

There comes a point when enough is enough. Every **new** project is a chance to hone your skills. Instead of spending hours on just **one** project, move on. When I have an email to send to our Brilliant Business Moms community, I generally write that email on Sunday nights. I know the deadline is approaching, but I don't want to spend all day on it. After dinner on Sundays, I sit down and write my email. I can generally complete it in thirty minutes or less.

If I used Friday naptime or Friday morning preschool time to write my email, I guarantee you my little perfectionist heart would find a reason to research email marketing for two hours, then spend another two hours crafting the perfect email - word for word. When I do this, I'm robbing our community of what they need so much more - a book on time management, or a new planner to help them reach their goals. In our weekly emails, they just want to hear from Sarah and I. They don't care if I write a beautiful thesis each week. *(And, let's be honest, they will probably be annoyed if I write a thesis every Sunday night!)*

If you prefer to work well in advance, but still want to maximize your productivity, you can employ a similar technique: Time yourself for each task. Give yourself twenty minutes to create a cover photo and nothing more. Race against the clock and you'll be amazed at how much you can complete when you work with focused intensity.

Our best work should be saved for the tasks that are the keystone of our businesses. In these cases, I do **not** recommend procrasti-planning or racing against the clock. What are those keystone tasks? They are different for every person. For example, spending hours on taking and improving photos may not be the most important task for a craft blogger, but it may be the most important task for a photographer who wants to book more weddings. Spending hours baking, refining, and re-baking cookies so the recipe is perfect may not be the most important task for a family-centered blogger, but it may be the most important task for a cookbook author. Only you can decide what those most-important tasks are. Keep your top five passions and great big goals in mind as you think through every item on your to-do list. For everything else - work quickly so that you can get back to what matters most.

Take-Aways

- Use the ten-minute rule to avoid procrastination. Tell yourself you must spend only ten minutes on your big goal, or ten minutes on that nagging task you've been avoiding, then get to work.
- Use the two-minute rule for tasks that pop into your mind throughout the day. If something takes just two minutes or less to complete, do it now rather than waste brain space trying to remember it for later.
- If you're a perfectionist, procrasti-planning may help you to curb your desire to spend hours on a simple project. Do the task right before its due to encourage focus and speed over perfection.
- Racing against the clock for easy tasks is another way to curb time-wasting behavior. Work with focused intensity for a set amount of time.

Chapter 16: Teach your Inbox to Sit, Lie Down, & Roll Over
-Sarah

There they were: 1,603 emails, just staring at me. Their beady little eyes begging for my attention. Important emails. Junk emails. Fun emails. SPAM emails. Emails from my sister. Emails selling me body wash. So. Many. Emails! Can you relate?

The 1,603 emails in my inbox wouldn't get the best of me this time. I may have started with 1,603 emails, but it only took me an hour and a half to get to inbox zero.

Are you ready to get to inbox zero?

Here's how to get it done: Keep your To Do List by your side while you are working on inbox zero. If something in an email must be dealt with or requires an action, write it down on your To Do List. I also made a folder called To Do for anything I would need to reference in the near future. Only put emails in a To Do folder if they are actually **on** your To Do list. I labeled this folder @ To Do so that it would appear at the top of my folder list.

Begin by searching for your highest frequency emails using your email search feature. When pages of emails from a particular sender come up as a search result, put them into an appropriate folder or delete them. Do not read them all. For instance, my biggest email sender is my sister, Beth Anne. When I did a search for emails from Beth Anne, 11 pages came up! Any emails prior to our podcast launch I put in a folder labeled Amateur Naturalist, because most likely those communications related to our Etsy shop. Any emails after the Podcast launch date probably relate to our podcast, so I selected those emails and placed them in a Brilliant Business Moms folder. Who needs to read 11 pages of emails from Beth Anne?! However, by placing the emails in folders, I have them for reference if ever needed. Continue this same process for all commonly recurring emails.

Make folders for anything you want to keep: mortgage documents, kids' sports, taxes, recipes, etc. Don't skimp on the number of folders. They need to be specific enough to make every email easy to find.

Don't read the emails - you can tell by the sender what they are about. Just get them into a folder or delete them.

I have folders for all of the kids' activities, which is really helpful. When a school lunch menu, or a Girl Scout email appears, I can do a quick scan, add necessary items to my To Do List, and keep the emails for reference in properly labeled folders. I don't need those emails clogging my inbox.

After you've searched for your most frequent email senders and created folders, you won't have too many emails left. Scan each page for any emails you want moved to a folder, once that is done, delete the entire page. Hopefully by this point it's a quick scan, and each page can be dealt with quickly.

Don't be distracted, keep working until you are done. It will feel so great to have the mess of your inbox defeated and put in its place!

These few steps are all it takes to get to inbox zero. Pretty painless, right? Once you get to inbox zero, how do you stay there? Emails flood in every single day!

There are a few strategies I use to stay at inbox zero. Most of the time my inbox is at 1 page, and that is working well for me. It's much better than 80 pages!

Set time aside to process your email each day, and like your paper inbox, after you process, there should be nothing left in your inbox. When you check your email, make sure you have time to deal with it immediately. Avoid checking your email if you only have 5 minutes. Five minutes is not enough time to read the email, update your To Do list, move emails into folders, and reply to emails. Your inbox is not your To Do list, so make sure you have your To Do list handy as you process emails.

Most productivity experts recommend that you only check email a few times a day. I'm trying to restrict email checking to 3 times per day and closing it for the rest of the day. This is tough to do, but important! It's a work in progress for me.

To make my inbox leaner and to quickly unsubscribe to email lists I don't want to receive any longer, I signed up for Unroll.me. Unroll.me makes unsubscribing as easy as clicking a button. Believe me, I unsubscribed from a lot! You can also choose to have Unroll.me "roll-up" all of your subscriptions into one email that you receive once a day. Their roll-up service has allowed me to scan through my subscriptions much more quickly. I have shaved so much time off of checking my email with their free service. A couple of months in with Unroll.me and they have unsubscribed me from 104 email subscriptions. These are email newsletters I was no longer reading, but hadn't take the time to unsubscribe from.

With a tamed inbox and a To Do List system that

is working, it feels like an enormous weight has been lifted off of me! *(Who knew?! I used to think emails were weightless... but now I know they're not!)*

Take-Aways

- Don't treat your inbox like a To Do list, actually use a To Do list.
- Push yourself to tame your inbox. You'll be much more productive with a streamlined system for tackling emails.
- Employ lots of folders to retain and easily find important emails.
- Avoid checking your email more than 3 times a day.
- When you do check your email, deal with everything at once instead of letting emails accumulate.

Chapter 17: Home Efficiencies -Sarah

A chapter like this would never fly in a male-dominated business book, but in a woman's real world, any efficiencies gained at home result in more time to spend on your business or with your family. I prefer to spend time on entrepreneurial endeavors or games with my kids rather than on housework. What about you?

I will never win a prize for pristine home of the year, but that's ok. I readily admit that my priorities for this time in my life are focused on family and business, with housework coming in nearly last. However, if you stopped by most days, I would welcome you into my home with only a slight cringe and apology. The house stays at an acceptable level at most times. Despite housework ranking low on my priority list, our home does run smoothly. We rarely have moments of panic and stress over schedules, supplies, groceries, dinner, clean laundry or the state of the home.

A home does need to be maintained at a level acceptable to you and your family. Your version of acceptable may be different from your friend's version, and that's ok. I do believe there is a lot of value in creating and maintaining a house that feels like "home". A crucial part of creating a welcoming home environment is cleanliness and order.

I absolutely love the sentiments expressed by Cheryl Mendelson in her book *Home Comforts.* "People used to be fond of the old saying that a housewife's work is never done, but you do not hear it much anymore, perhaps because today, so often, the housewife's work is never started. In any event, this maxim, like most, is only half true. Yes, you can always think of something else that could be done, and yes, you will do more tomorrow, but in fact there really is an end to what your routine calls for this day or week or year. You, however, are the one who sets limits...In my experience, the most common cause of dislike of housework is the feeling that the work is never done, that it never gives a sense of satisfaction...To avoid this, you have to decide what ordinary, daily level of functioning you want in your home. There ought to be a word for this level, but there isn't... Whatever words you use, you need to create end points that will let you . . . say to yourself "Finished!" Otherwise you will feel trapped and resentful . . ." [26]

If you practice some of the principles discussed in the time-blocking chapter, you should have a loose plan for when housework happens, but we still want to get it done as quickly as possible. Let's discuss a few small ways to be more efficient at housework. There is nothing groundbreaking here, but you may discover something you haven't thought about in a while.

Errands

Shopping and errands can really break up your day and be a time-waster if you're not careful. An organized list of errands is the first step to reigning in trips to the store. I use a whiteboard on my fridge to keep a running grocery list as well as items I might need from Target or Home Depot, including any items that need to be returned to those stores. When I'm headed to a particular store, I check the whiteboard.

Efficiency with errands can be done in several ways. Running errands all in one day may work for the mom who has older kids, or children in school. If your child's preschool is far away or just for a short time, running errands during preschool hours probably makes sense. Beth Anne never does errands while her son Holden is in preschool so that she doesn't have to use up her alone time. Instead she uses preschool hours as quality work time and does errands with Holden later. He chatters away and says hi to everyone in the store, and he likes being out and about on his non-preschool days!

There is no perfect formula for any mom, but running an errand every single day is not going to be the most efficient use of your time. The more you are home, the more you can accomplish in your business or on housework.

Cheri Tracy of Orglamix.com swears by Amazon Prime. She orders everything from toilet paper to office supplies to a new kitchen faucet. For Cheri, she feels it saves money and time, and cuts down on the number of errands she has to run.

Laundry

Most bloggers seem to advocate the load-of-laundry-every-day plan. I find this to be quite inefficient and Cheryl Mendelson agrees. The more you stay on the same track, doing the same thing, the more efficient you are. Grouping tasks saves time. [26] *(It's so fun having a housekeeping guru on my side!)*

I like to do three loads in one morning, and then fold them all at once. I start with towels and underwear because being a little wrinkled from waiting to be folded won't matter, and I end with a load that I would not want to be wrinkled, and fold that first. All the laundry is taken to my bedroom, and I turn on a podcast or audio book while I fold. I look forward to folding laundry because I know I can listen to something I enjoy while I work!

By the end of the folding session, everything is in piles on the bed, and it has to be put away before I can go to sleep that night. This eliminates baskets of laundry lying around the house. When the kids are getting ready for bed, they come and grab their piles of laundry and put them away. Just like that, laundry is done!

Another way to be more efficient at laundry is

to make less of it. This may gross you out, but here goes! Are your jeans really that dirty from sitting at the computer writing blog posts all day? Maybe they could be worn another day before being laundered. Maybe the blouse your little girl wore to her choir concert can be worn to church next Sunday without a wash and dry. Did the kids by some strange miracle manage to make it through the day without getting anything on their pants? They can wear them again! Cleanliness is important, but we probably wash clothes just because they were worn for a while and not because they are actually dirty or stinky.

Cleaning

Grouping housekeeping activities like cleaning toilets or sinks, can help you save time and stay on top of cleaning. Maybe you don't have time to clean all the bathrooms top to bottom, but you do have 10 minutes to clean all the toilets. By using the same tools to do the same activity throughout the house, you are more efficient than using that same 10 minutes to clean different items in the same bathroom. Using just 10 minutes to do a quick clean instead of wasting 10 minutes on twitter can make a huge difference in your ability to stay on top of your housework.

Keep cleaning tools and cleaning agents both

upstairs and downstairs to save time and energy. If you have a few minutes to clean a bedroom, you won't have to chase down cleaning supplies from all over the house. A second vacuum stored upstairs may be a luxury item worth investigating.

Amy Gabriel of GabrielsGoodTidings.Etsy.com cleans the sink and toilet while she is keeping an eye on her kids in the bathtub, and Barbara Leyne of BarbaraLeyne.com cleans the shower while she's in the shower!

Rewarding myself is another tool I use to push myself to clean the house. I tell myself, after you do x, y, z then you can read 2 chapters in your book. A reward at the other end of the task helps me push through and work as fast as I can. In addition, when I get my reward it feels so good! If I would have just sat down and read, it wouldn't have been as pleasant because I would still be thinking about those unfinished tasks. It's a beautiful system: More is accomplished, and the reward feels sweeter because it's well-earned.

Using a timer for you and your kids can be another great way to really knock out some household chores. It can be so defeating to see a gigantic mess. It's tempting to just skip picking up anything at all. A 10 minute burst of collective or singular effort in a messy room can make a huge difference. Have you ever noticed how quickly you can get the house looking in much better shape if a friend calls to say she wants to stop by in 10 minutes? To motivate yourself during these short bursts of cleaning, just pretend your friend is about to drop by!

To motivate the kids, I like to plan our 10 minute rapid pick-up right before their favorite show. I encourage the kids to work hard or they might have to miss a few minutes of their show. Making the 10 minute clean-up part of our daily routine makes a huge difference. Sometimes I verbally award someone the honor of best cleaner for that time. They really get serious about picking up if they think their brother or sister will beat them for this coveted award!

Training Children

I'm trying to train the children to pick up after themselves as they go. This has been a tough one! Wrappers and garbage left in the family room drives me crazy! I would be embarrassed to admit how many partially decaying pieces of fruit I have found stashed in various places in the house! My kids are old enough to know not to leave garbage lying around, and we have talked with them about this on many occasions. When they have gone upstairs to play, but left their garbage in the family room, I intentionally call them from their play to throw away their garbage. I make it inconvenient in hopes that someday they realize that it's easier to just clean up right away.

Teaching children to do chores is an important part of their training, but so often it seems easier for you to do it. This may be true in the short term, but after some training and teaching, you will have children who can do many things without your involvement.

Think of your household like a workplace. If a boss never trained an employee to do their job, the boss would end up doing their job plus the job of the employee and the employee would never learn needed skills. By investing time early on to train the employee, the boss gains thousands of work hours for his small investment and the employee gains knowledge. I know kids aren't our employees, but the principle holds true, especially applied with warmth, love, and affection

My kids enjoy cleaning - especially if it involves spraying, water, bubbles, or wipes. Tasks they love to do are cleaning windows, wiping doorknobs, cleaning the banister, or wiping out a sink. My friend Diane enlists her daughter, age 7, to wipe down the baseboards. I don't know why I hadn't thought of that one yet! Baseboards almost never get done in our house, and my kids would love using water to clean them. Not to mention, it's easier for them because they are closer to the floor with more flexibility than me!

The Swiffer Wet Jet is not the most economical choice when it comes to mopping but my kids like to use it. In the end, mopping gets done even if it's not perfect or the most cost-efficient method. A little mopping, imperfectly done and a little pricey, but the end result is a child who is proud . . . they helped!

Antibacterial wipes are another cleaning supply they love to use, but they really aren't the most frugal cleaning tool. However, germs get eradicated by the kids, so I call that a win.

Lauree Sayne of DancingDishandDecor.Etsy.com shared a tip her mom used. "At night we all had to give her 15 minutes of cleaning time - not cleaning our rooms, but helping to clean the common areas of the house. Another thing she did was instead of just grounding us or putting us in the corner, we had to clean something. I remember using Q-tips to clean the crevices of the end tables. You would think it would make your kids hate cleaning, but it gave me time to think about why I was being punished and it gave me a sense of accomplishment."

Don't be afraid to challenge your kids! In the summer, the girls do their own laundry, with a little help from me. This developed because the number of outfit changes was driving me crazy! The girls would put perfectly clean clothes down the laundry shoot! My son (4) is actually pretty decent at vacuuming. These jobs are not done perfectly, and do require a bit of my time, but the end result is that things are cleaner than when we started. Maybe they're not as clean and neat as if I had done them, but that's the point, I didn't have to do them!

Cooking

Cooking is a huge part of every mom's day. If we counted up the number of hours we spend in the kitchen making and preparing food for our most important charges, it would be thousands! There are ways that we can still provide great meals for our family while saving time too.

Freezer cooking is one of the most efficient ways I know of to consistently serve healthy homemade meals to your family. If you have never tried freezer cooking before, I recommend Jessica Fisher's book, *Not Your Mother's Make Ahead and Freeze Cookbook* (goodcheapeats.com). It's my go-to book for freezer recipes. Freezer cooking is preparing multiple meals at one time so that they can be stored in your freezer and pulled out for a future meal. Freezer cooking can be done in a couple of ways.

Some people have a marathon day of freezer cooking and make enough meals to last several weeks or even a month. The other method of freezer cooking is to make larger batches of the meal you are cooking for that evening's dinner and freeze the rest for a future meal. When I make Jessica Fisher's Chicken Divan recipe, I make enough for three batches. One batch is for that evening, and the other two are frozen.

Freezer cooking is very time efficient. First, you only shop for ingredients once. Second, you are doing food prep all at one time. Cooking and dicing 3 pounds of chicken takes hardly any more time than cooking and dicing 1 pound of chicken. Third, you create a messy kitchen only once.

Counters are scrubbed and cleaned once instead of three times. Cutting boards, utensils, and dishes are cleaned just once as well.

If you haven't tried freezer cooking, give it a try. It's an amazing feeling to have a freezer full of homemade meals for dinner instead of stopping mid-project to figure out what to make for dinner.

Dana Regehr of JanieLaneStudio.Etsy.com agrees, "Having freezer meals stocked is the BEST feeling. Because my boys are young, I can mostly split a 9 x 13 casserole into two 8 x 8s and freeze one."

Julie Fuller of TokyoBlossom.Etsy.com says, "I have been using my crock pot more than ever for meals...,"

While we're in the kitchen, I have a new, perhaps devious "trick" I just discovered. My husband Mike always helps me clean the kitchen after dinner. I try to run the dishwasher before dinner even if it isn't quite full. After dinner, we unload the dishwasher together and then we load the dishwasher with dishes from our evening meal. This method leaves zero dirty dishes in the sink.

Mike's help saves me clean-up time, and we talk about our day as we work and enjoy a few moments together. This little trick never dawned on me before because the money-saving frugal side of me always waited until the dishwasher was completely full to run it. Missing out on a plate being washed isn't going to break the bank, and my time is worth more. By running the dishwasher a little ahead of schedule, I get help cleaning the entire kitchen and enjoy chatting with my husband while we work.

My friend Gretchen reserves electronics for her children when she is cooking dinner. She can cook uninterrupted but doesn't feel guilty about the electronics because the kids haven't been using them all day. An added benefit is that the kids are more distracted with electronics than with other toys, and so they don't complain about being hungry and wanting a snack. It helps save their appetite for dinner. Perfect!

Minimalism and Frugality

I know in my head that the more "stuff" I have the longer my housework takes. It takes time to organize all the stuff, clean the stuff, and put the stuff away. I am doing my best to purge more and let go of as much stuff as possible, but it's taking time. It is easy for me to get stressed that I am not making more progress in that area, but all of this stuff didn't come into the house in one day, and it's not all going to leave the house in one day either. It's a process, but by keeping the idea of simplicity front- of-mind, I continue to make progress and reassess which things our family uses and needs.

I keep two boxes in my garage, one for garage sale items and one for items to donate. When the purging mood strikes I can either toss the item in the garbage or place it in one of my boxes.

I have always tended towards frugality. I love garage sales and thrift stores. For a long time I was an avid coupon clipper and deal shopper. I washed plastic bags and saved foil. All of this is good, but now I realize that my time is more valuable to me than the money saved in some instances. It has been hard for me to give up some of my frugal ways, but slowly I am realizing that sometimes more time is better than 50 cents in my pocket.

Coupon cutting is one thing that I've decided to stop entirely. My coupon cutting had been on a slow decline for a while, but I've finally decided I'm done with grocery store coupons. I'm done with washing plastic bags too, at least for a little while. However, shopping at the discount grocery store right next to the preschool -- yes to that! Stocking up on groceries when they are on sale -- that I can easily keep doing.

You will still find me at garage sales and thrift

stores because I love doing that for fun. Hand-me -down clothes for the kids -- send them my way! Buying a used car, I'm there. Saving foil...I think I'll recycle it. Am I still going to be mindful of my money? Absolutely. Set a budget with my husband? You bet. I'm just giving myself permission to switch gears toward saving time over money when it makes sense. Up until now, I hadn't been willing to give myself that permission.

Traditional Roles

Another reason our home runs efficiently is because Mike and I are willing to cross lines when it comes to traditional male/female household jobs.

Mike usually takes out the garbage, but if I know he's working late, he wouldn't be at all surprised to come home and find that I had taken the garbage to the curb. Mike usually mows the lawn, but this summer when he was remodeling our kitchen, I mowed the lawn so he could keep working. Speaking of the kitchen, I helped lay the floor and built a bench with my dad to go underneath the window. I'm actually quite proud of the fact that I don't mind, and even enjoy swinging a hammer or pulling the trigger on the nail gun!

Mike is equally as good about jumping in and doing household chores. If I am particularly busy one week, he'll do the laundry on the weekend. When he's home on weekends, he often does all the dishes. I don't have to ask. He jumps in on whatever needs to be done around the house. I know Beth Anne and Chris also operate this way. When he is deployed, she is the only one around to handle everything. I have seen Chris in action sweeping floors and folding laundry. Because we are both willing to work on any chore, our home runs much more smoothly.

Any small step toward greater household efficiency will give you more time to focus on your family and business. So let's get this housework done!

Take-Aways

- Staying on top of housework is the most efficient way to run a house.
- Any efficiencies gained on housework leaves more time for your big goal, business, and family.
- Take one tip at a time and try it out. Nothing will be gained without taking action!

AFTERWORD

Time-management is a topic that could be covered.... until the end of time! This certainly hasn't been an exhaustive study of time management, but we hope you've walked away with several practical applications to make better use of the margins in your day as a busy mom.

These methods have worked well for us, and we've seen them make a difference for other moms too. Since we're all about using your time well, we won't keep you any longer! It's time to get out there and pursue those passions while parenting with intention! You got this!

Feel free to use the hashtag #timemgmtmama on Instagram or Twitter if you need support or want to share big wins! We love hearing from you!

You can follow us on social media @brilliantbizmom or BrilliantBusinessMoms on most platforms.

Here's to your most productive year ever!
We can't wait to see what you accomplish!

~ **Sarah Korhnak and**
Beth Anne Schwamberger

WORKS CITED

S. Dinsmore, "LiveYourLegend.Net," 1 February 2011. [Online]. Available: http://liveyourlegend.net/warren-buffetts-5-step-process-for-prioritizing-true-success-and-why-most-people-never-do-it/. [Accessed 15 May 2015].

A. L. Andrews, Tell Your Time: How to Manage Your Schedule so you can Live Free, Amy Lynn Andrews, 2011.

D. Allen, Getting Things Done, The Art of Stress-Free Productivity, New York: Penguin Books, 2001.

D. Allen, in *Getting Things Done, The Art of Stress-Free Productivity,* New York, Penguin Books, 2001.

K. Clemons, S. Korhnak and B. A. Schwamberger, "The Importance of Story-Telling with Katie Clemons of Gadanke," 19 August 2014. [Online]. Available: http://www.brilliantbusinessmoms.com/storytelling-katie-clemons-gadanke/. [Accessed 15 May 2015].

P. Flynn, "Smart Passive Income," 22 December 2010. [Online]. Available: http://www.smartpassiveincome.com/spi-012-mind-hacks-physical-hacks-and-work-hacks-for-better-productivity-and-getting-things-done/. [Accessed 15

May 2015].

S. Korhnak and B. A. Schwamberger, "Blogging your Passion + E-books with Kristen, the Frugal Girl," 8 September 2014. [Online]. Available: http://www.brilliantbusinessmoms.com/kristen-the-frugal-girl/ . [Accessed 15 May 2015].

LifeHacker, "LifeHacker," 2007 24 July. [Online]. Available: Source: http://lifehacker.com/281626/jerry-seinfelds-productivity-secret. [Accessed 15 May 2015].

C. Paine, "MoneySavingMom.com," 1 December 2014. [Online]. Available: http://moneysavingmom.com/2014/12/d-o-n-e.html. [Accessed 15 May 2015].

S. Korhnak, B. A. Schwamberger and C. Starr-Rose, "Brilliant Business Moms," 11 November 2014. [Online]. Available: http://www.brilliantbusinessmoms.com/getting-published-author-caroline-starr-rose/. [Accessed 15 May 2015].

N. Barry, "The Nathan Barry Show," 25 September 2014. [Online]. Available: Source: http://nathanbarry.com/episode11/. [Accessed 15 May 2015].

S. Korhnak, S. Mackenzie and B. A. Schwamberger, "3000 Book Sales + 1 Million Ideas with Sarah Mackenzie," 16 December 2014. [Online]. Available: http://www.brilliantbusinessmoms.com/3000-book-sales-1-million-ideas-sarah-mackenzie/. [Accessed 15 May 2015].

TerKeurst, The Best Yes: Making Wise Decisions in the Midst of Endless Demands, Nashville: Thomas Nelson Publishers, 2014.

M. Thomas, H. Sing, H. Holcomb, H. Mayberg, R. Dannals, H. Wagner, D. Thorne, K. Popp, L. Rowland, A. Welsh and S. R. D. Balwinski, "Neural basis of alertness and cognitive performance impairments during sleepiness. I. Effects of 24 h of sleep deprivation on waking human regional brain activity," *Journal of Sleep Research,* vol. 9, no. 4, pp. 335-352, 2000.

L. S. Talbot, E. L. McGlinchey, K. A. Kaplan, R. E. Dahl and A. G. Harvey, "Sleep deprivation in adolescents and adults: Change in affect," *Emotion,* vol. 10, no. 6, pp. 831-841, 2010.

C. A. C. G. M. F. M. C. D. G. L. F. M. Tempesta Daniela, "Lack of sleep affects the evaluation of emotional stimuli," *Brain Research Bulletin,* vol. 82, no. 1-2, pp. 104-108, 2010.

M.-P. St-Onge, A. L. Roberts, J. Chen, M. Kelleman, M. O'Keeffee, A. RoyChoudhury and P. J. Jones, "Short sleep duration increases energy intakes but does not change energy expenditure in normal-weight individuals," *American Journal of Clinical Nutrition,* vol. 94, no. 2, pp. 410-416, 2011.

G. McKeown, Essentialism: The Disciplined Pursuit

of Yes, New York: Crown Publishing Group, 2014.

A. A. o. Pedicatrics and R. Moon, Sleep: What Every Parent Needs to Know, Elk Grove Village: The American Academy of Pediatrics, 2013.

M. Meeker and L. Wu, "Internet Trends," Kleiner, Perkins, Caulfield & Byers, Menlo Park, 2013.

American Psychological Association, "Multitasking: Switching costs," 20 March 2006. [Online]. Available: http://www.apa.org/research/action/multitask.aspx. [Accessed 16 May 2015].

G. J. Mark, S. Voida and A. V. Cardello, "A Pace Not Dictated by Electrons: An Empirical STudy of Work Without Email," Association for Computing Machinery, Austin, 2012.

G. B. Armstrong and L. Chung, "Background Television and Reading Memory in Context: Assessing TV Interference and Facilitative Context Effects on Encoding Versus Retrieval Processes," *Communication Research,* vol. 27, no. 3, pp. 327-352, 2000.

E. Ophir and C. W. A. D. Nass, "Cognitive Control in Media Multitaskers," *Proceedings of the National Academy of Sciences of the United States of America,* vol. 106, no. 37, pp. 15583-15587, 2009.

A. Bogel, "Modern Mrs. Darcy," 17 April 2014. [Online]. Available: http://modernmrsdarcy.com/2014/04/the-secret-to-faking-a-clean-house/. [Accessed 16 May 2015].

Made in the USA
Columbia, SC
09 March 2018

C. Mendelson, Home Comforts: The Art and Science of Keeping House, New York: Simon and Schuster, 2005.

www.BrilliantBusinessMoms.com